Historical and Statistical Abstract of the Colony of Hongkong

HISTORICAL

AND

STATISTICAL ABSTRACT

OF THE

COLONY

OF

HONGKONG.

HONGKONG:
PRINTED BY NORONHA & Co.
Government Printers
1911.
Ke

First Preface

The *Principal Events* and notes on *Trade and Industry* for the period prior to the close of Sir John Pope Hennessy's administration in March, 1882, have been taken largely from Dr E J Eitel's History of Hongkong The information under these headings subsequent to that date has been mainly extracted from official publications The notes on *Public Works* have been furnished by the Director of that department In the brief summary of *Legislation* the Ordinances in force at the end of 1901 have been given the numbers they bear in Sir John Carrington's edition

Under the heading *Trade* the figures dealing with *ships cleared and entered* exclude steam-launches and junks whether engaged in foreign or local trade The excess in numbers of *emigrants returned* over *emigrants left* is accounted for by many that leave from various Treaty Ports of China returning *via* Hongkong

Under *Finance* the percentage of expenditure devoted to *Non-effective Charges* is based on the inclusion under that head of Pensions and Interest *General Administration* covers the Governor's Office, the Colonial Secretary's, Registrar General's and Audit Departments, the Treasury, the Post Office, the Harbour Department, the Observatory, Charitable Allowances, Transport and Miscellaneous Services *Law and Order* include the Supreme Court, Magistracy, Law Officers, Land Registry, Police, Fire Brigade and Gaol The Botanical and Afforestation as well as the Medical and Sanitary Departments are included under *Public Health* *Public Instruction* comprises the Education Department, Queen's College and Ecclesiastical Allowances *Public Works* covers the Public Works establishment as well as annually recurrent and extraordinary works *Defence* includes the Military Contribution and Volunteers

The statistics given under *Climate* were obtained from various sources prior to 1884 when the Observatory at Kowloon was established

The *Population* statistics prior to 1869 are exclusive and for that and subsequent years inclusive of the Army and Navy in the Colony Except for the years 1904 and 1905, when the population of New Kowloon, i e, of the New Territories South of the Kowloon Hills, is included, these statistics do not take those Territories into consideration The population of the New Territories according to the Census taken in 1901 was 102,254 of which 17,243 were in New Kowloon

Under *Public Instruction* the figures given from the year 1875 onward show the number of Grant-in-Aid Schools in place of the number of Mission Schools and the average daily attendance in place of the total number of scholars as the progress of education is considered to be thereby more correctly indicated. In the earlier years the total number of schools under European supervision and of scholars enrolled in them are alone available.

The statistics under the heading *Public Order* require no comment. Those under *Defence* referring to regular troops are taken from returns by the Principal Medical Officer.

M. NATHAN

GOVERNMENT HOUSE,
December, 1906

Second Preface.

In 1910 it was decided that the Historical and Statistical Abstract, being a most useful record for reference should be printed as a separate publication once in every 10 years, the unexpired decade only appearing in the Civil Service List, the first issue of this separate record to be compiled and published in 1911 —up to and including 1910.

Under "Finance" a new sub-head has been added for 1910, "Undertakings of Government." This column includes the Post Office and Kowloon-Canton Railway. Previously the Post Office had been included in "General Administration."

To the Departments under "Public Order" has been added 'District Office'. A District Officer was appointed for the New Territories on 23rd September, 1907.

Queen's College is no longer a separate Department. On 20th May, 1909, the Secretary of State approved of its being brought under the Education Department.

The Army and Navy and the New Territories have been included in the figures shown under "Population" since the year 1907. The figures given are approximate only —except for the years in which a census has been taken.

F. D. LUGARD

GOVERNMENT HOUSE,
1st April, 1911.

(1.)—HISTORY

PRINCIPAL EVENTS, TRADE AND INDUSTRIES, PUBLIC WORKS, LEGISLATION.

Abbreviations

Pr Ev —Principal Events   P. W —Public Works.
Tr & Ind —Trade & Industries   H K —Hongkong

1841.

Captain Charles Elliot, R N , administered from 26 1 1841 to 10 8.1841

Pr. Ev.—H K is taken over (26/1) and Govt administered by Capt ELLIOT as Chief Superintendent of the Trade of Br. subjects in China in accordance with proclamation issued by him (29/1), which also declared that Chinese should be governed according to laws of China and others according to laws of Gt Britain 2nd proclamation (1/2) promised free exercise of religious rites, social customs and private rights Br and foreign merchants came from Macao to prospect (Feb) Building commenced (March). Messrs Jardine, Matheson & Co. erected first substantial house and godowns at East Point. Military and naval establishments first located near West Point and mercantile centre at Wong Nei Cheong Valley but this proved too unhealthy Chinese settled to W of this valley in "the Canton Bazaar" and near site of later Central Market in "the Bazaar". About 2,000 Tan ka or boat people came to Colony In 1st issue of *H K Govt Gozette* (1/5) Ch Magistrate appointed and in 2nd issue (15/5) original census published Proclamation of 7/6 declared H K a free port At 1st sale of lands, subsequently disallowed, 33 marine lots aggregating about 9 acres sold for total annual rent of £3,032 Outbreak of malignant malarial fever in June, violent typhoons on 21-22 & 25 26/7 and destructive fire on 12/8 retarded progress of new Colony Harbour Master, Clerk of Works, Colonial Surgeon and Land Officer appointed

1842.

Sir Henry Pottinger, Bart , G C B , in charge of Government from 11 8 1841 to 25 6 1843 , Governor 26 6 1843 to 7 5 1844
(Mr A. R Johnston administered during the latter half of 1841 and 1842)

Pr. Ev.—Establishment of Superintendent of Trade moved from Macao to H K (27/2) Treaty of Nanking (29/8) confirmed cession of H K On conclusion of war fleet and troops, except garrison of 700, left and arrangements made to bring local affairs under Col Office, Superintendency of Trade, held by Gov , still remaining under Foreign Office Post Office organized Committee appointed (29/3) to investigate claims to land and lay out town , main street called Queen's Road Baptist Chapel opened there (7/7) "Friend of China" newspaper established (17/3) **Tr. & Ind** —Mexican and other Republican dollars declared to be standard in all matters of trade (27/4) **P. W.**—Barracks erected on Cantonment Hill, at Stanley and at Aberdeen Central Market, subsequently removed to site on other side of Queen's Road, opened (10/6) Road constructed from Wong Nei Cheong to Shau Ki Wan

1843.

Pr. Ev --Following on Royal Warrant appointing the Chief Superintendent of Trade, Sir HENRY POTTINGER, to be Gov & C in C of the Colony of H K and its Dependencies, Col Govt was organized with a Lieut Gov, Col Sec, Treasurer Chinese Sec, Legal Advisor, Col Surgeon, Col Chaplain, Ch Magist, Harbour Mr, Col Surveyor and Land Officer, and Postmaster Also 18 officials and 26 unofficials appointed J s of P City named "Victoria" (29/6) Col Chaplain first officiated in matshed church (24/12), he started St Paul's College for training Chinese to be C of D ministers R C church in Wellington Street consecrated (18/6) Mosque built Morrison Education Society, transferred from Macao, opened school on Morrison Hill (11/1) Hosps. established by Med Missionary Society and by naval and milit authorities Health very bad, between May and Oct 24% of troops and 10% of European civilians died of fever Committee of Public Health and Cleanliness appointed Attempts made to check land jobbing **Tr. & Ind.**—At end of year 12 large English firms, 10 English merchants on smaller scale and about 6 Indian firms As a result of peace junk trade declined and opening of 5 treaty ports including Shanghai (11/1) adversely affected trade of H K First H K built vessel "The Celestial" of 80 tons launched from patent slip at E Point (7/2) **Leg.**—Royal Instructions of 6/4 constituted Ex and Leg Councils, each of 3 members exclusive of Gov

1844

Governor Sir John Francis Davis, Bart, (8 5 1844 to 18 3 1848)
(Major-General G C D'Aguilar administered on various occasions)

Pr Ev.—Attempt to regulate population by Registration Ord opposed at first public meeting in H K (28/10) and by general strike (30/10) Supreme Court opened (1/10) Police force organized (1/5) At land sale on 22/1 101 lots aggregating 25ac sold for £2,562 annual rental Anglo-Ch College for training Ch ministers opened by London Miss Soc Seamen's Hosp built by public subscription (30 9) Tai Ping Shan Market started Amateur Dramatic Club formed (18/12) **Tr. & Ind.**--Trade except in opium declined, partly owing to restrictions imposed by Ch authorities under Sir H POTTINGER'S Supplementary Treaty of 8/10/43 Piracy round H K also affected junk trade First opium ord passed (26/11) and farm let for $720 p m Salt tax instituted **Leg.**—First sitting of Leg Council (11/1) Land Registration Ord (No 1) established office for registration of conveyance of realty and made provision for security of titles

1845.

Pr. Ev—Police rates introduced and house property rated after some opposition Consul for U S A appointed (12/11) P & O S N Co started monthly mail steamers (1/8) School for English children and Union Church opened "China Mail" newspaper started (20/2) **Tr. & Ind.**—Attempt made to put currency on gold basis soon failed Branch of Oriental Bank Corporation established (April) Opium farm let for $1,710 p m ". W.— Wong Nei Cheong Valley drained, road made round it, and colonial cemetery with chapel opened Road constructed from Shau Ki Wan to Tytam (5 3 m) 3 landing Piers on City front and 3 Police Stations in City built Temporary Govt Ho completed (11/1) **L g.**—Summary Offences Ord (No 1) passed

1846.

Pr. Ev.—Much friction between judicial and executive branches of Govt Vice-Admiralty Court established (4/3) Consuls for Denmark and Portugal appointed (11 & 12/3) H K Club opened (26/5) **Tr. & Ind.**—Junk trade revived Attempt of merchants to obtain protection for tea shipped at H K failed Opium farm let $1,560 p m

1847.

Pr. Ev—Sir J Davis made ineffectual milit expedition to Canton (2/4 to 8/4) to secure fulfilment of terms of Nanking Treaty of 1842 Also failed in attempt to establish commercial relations with Annam (Oct) Difficulties between judicial and executive branches of Govt culminated in trial of Ch Justice by Ex Council (22/11) Parliamentary Comm appointed (March) to enquire into commercial relations in China reported adversely on monopolies, petty regulations and expensive establishment in H K Milit authorities decided to erect defensible barracks at Stanley (8/3) Foundation stone of St John's Cathedral laid (11/3) China Branch of Royal Asiatic Soc organized (15/1) Court ho purchased from Dent & Co **Tr. & Ind.**—Licences substituted for opium farm **P. W.**—Magistracy, Victoria Gaol (reconstructed in 1865) and Police Stations at Queen's Road East (now abolished) and at Aberdeen (since superseded) constructed 2,440 yards of City drains laid

1848.

Governor Sir Samuel George Bonham, G C B , (20 3 1818 to 12 4 1854).
(Major-General Staveley, C B , administered on various
occasions up to 25 2 1851)

Pr. Ev. —Large excess of expenditure over revenue required reduction in establishments and stoppage of P W Colonial Hosp oragnized (1/10) 13 vessels lost in typhoon (31/8-1/9) Amateur Dramatic Club revived (2/12) **Tr & Ind.**—Opening up of goldfields in Sacramento Valley initiated commerce and coolie emigration to San Francisco which grew rapidly in following years H K & Canton Steam Packet Co. established (19,10) **P. W.**—Govt Offices near Cathedral and Court house in Queen's Road completed and road from Aberdeen to Stanley (6¾ m) constructed

1849.

Pr. Ev—Hien Fung became Emperor of China (25/2) Sir G. Bonham's interview with Viceroy Sen (17/2) failed to gain permission for merchants to enter Canton City 83 pirate junks destroyed (Oct) 15 Justices of Peace selected by Gov to advise him Commission of enquiry into land tenure appointed (Oct) St John's Cathedral opened (11/3) and placed under Bishop of Victoria created by Letters Patent of 11/5. Various missionary schools including the one for English children had to be closed for want of support Victoria Regatta Club formed (25/10) **Tr. & Ind**—P & O S N Co commenced running regular steamer between H K and Shanghai **Leg** —Various Ords connected with administration of justice passed this year were superseded later.

1850.

Pr. Ev —Revolt originating in Kwang Si afterwards developed into Tai Ping rebellion   13 pirate junks destroyed in Mirs Bay (4/3)   136 men of 59th Regt died out of strength of 568, mostly from fever   Plague broke out in Canton in May but did not spread to H K   London Mission Hosp closed for want of funds   First Bishop—G Smith—arrived (29/3), became chairman of Educational Committee which administered Govt grants to schools and took charge of St Paul's College   Tr & Ind —Attempt of Canton Hoppo to prevent H K river steamers carrying cargo from H K to Canton checked   Leg.—Two unofficial members nominated by J s of P to Leg Council which previously consisted of 3 officials exclusive of Governor

1851

Major-General Jervois, K G , administered on various occasions between February 1851 and April 1854

Pr Ev —Discussion between Govt & J s of P re Municipal Govt which had been going on since 1849 led to no result   London Missionary Society opened chapel for treatment of out-patients (May)   472 houses North of Queen's Road destroyed by fire   Cricket Club established (June)   P. W —5 wells sunk for City Water Supply   Road from Albany Godowns to Wong Nei Cheong (now called Wan Chai Road) constructed and first Praya reclamation scheme partly carried out

1852.

Pr. Ev —Disturbances in S China incident on Tai Ping rebellion sent many Chinese to H K   19 cases of piracy in H K waters   Tr & Ind —Great increase in emigration to Straits Settlements and California   Emigration to Peru also benefited H K for a time till abuses connected with its trade necessitated abandonment   Coinage of Br dollar first mooted on account of Mex dollars, Ind rupees and Br coins being at a discount   P & O S N Co established regular monthly steamer between H K and Calcutta thereby giving Colony fortnightly communication with England   Exchange at 6 months' sight stood at 4 10½ a 5/- on December 30th

1853.

Pr. Ev —Shortlived Tai Ping dynasty established at Nanking visited by Sir G. Bonham who decided no liberal policy to be expected from it   Piratical fleet destroyed (10/5), nevertheless 70 cases of piracy during year including that of S S "Aratoon Apcar" (5/8)   Attempt to revive school for English children failed   Tr & Ind —Emigration to Br Guiana put on regular footing and that to Australia commenced   Chinese Govt. legalised importation of opium   Exchange at 6 months' sight stood at 5/- on December 29th   P. W.—Wong Nei Cheong Police Stn , Police Stn No 9 in Caine Road and 2 slaughter houses constructed, all subsequently abolished   Leg —Ord No 1 made it lawful for aliens to hold and transfer real property

— 5 —

1854

Governor Sir John Bowring, Kt, LL D, (13 4 1854 to 5 5 1859)
(Colonel W Caine administered on various occasions up to 8 9 1859)

Fr Ev —Kowloon City and other towns to N E of H K taken and re-taken by Tai Pings and Imperialists Rebels blockaded Canton River and threatened city, many Chinese taking refuge in H K (Dec) On outbreak of Crimean war batteries erected for defence of Colony 73 soldiers stricken with fever and dysentery in one month 6 cases of beri-beri, previously unknown in H K, occurred among Ind troops Tr & Ind —Emigration to Jamaica started (Nov) Opening of Japan by convention of 11/10 had little immediate though important ultimate effect on H K trade H K and Canton Steam Packet Co broke up (13/12) P. W —Wong Nei Cheong School (26 scholars) completed, afterwards given up

1855.

Pr. Ev.—Tai Ping and Imperialist fleets of war junks ordered out of H K harbour (Jan) Rebels retired from Canton river before Br force sent from H K Sir J Bowring failed to get recognition of this service from Viceroy Yeh Commission enquired into administration of Police force (Aug) 800 deaths among Chinese from fever between 6.2 & 28/4 Serious conflagration in centre of town (16 2) St Andrew's school for Br children established but failed after a few years Tr & Ind — Sir J Bowring's treaty with Siam started trade between H K and that country 3 new ports in Philippine Is opened P. W.—Parya scheme which re-established crown rights over reclaimed foreshore in front of town opposed by European lot-holders (5/12) Leg.—Leg Council increased to 3 unofficial and 6 official members

1856.

Pr Ev.—Anti-foreign placards and hostility of officials in Canton culminated in arrest there of Chinese crew of H K Lorcha "Arrow" Surrender and apology refused by Viceroy and forts and official residences in Canton bombarded without result except destruction of European Canton and Whampoa factories by Chinese mob S of S refused to consider proposal (17/4) to license gambling houses Serious fires at Tai Ping Shan (27/1) and Western Market (23/2) Volunteer Fire Brigade (23/1) and Chinese Fire Brigade (7/3) organized Govt. Ho completed Villas and farms established at Pok Fu Lam Anglo-Chinese College closed at end of year Leg —Ord No 1 authorized recognition of Chinese wills in local courts

1857.

Pr. Ev.—S S s "Feima" and "Thistle" captured by Chinese soldiers (Jan) 400 Europeans poisoned with arsenic believed to have been introduced into bakery at instance of Chinese officials (15/I), great excitement caused thereby in H K and in England led to Lord Elgin superseding Sir J Bowring as plenipotentiary in China and to "Arrow" war with that country, which was not however prosecuted during year owing to Ind mutiny France joined Gr Br and ultimatum issued to Viceroy (24/12) 32 cases of piracy between 1/11/56 and 15/2/57, afterwards decreased Local educational movement at low ebb Tr & Ind —Junk trade fell off owing to blockade of Canton River New docks established at Aberdeen (June) P W —Three Police Stations erected Praya scheme partly carried out Town now lighted by 350 oil lamps (1/10) Central Police Station finished Leg —Three official and one unofficial members added to Leg Council

1858

Pr Ev.—Canton captured by allied forces (5/1) and administered till 21/10/61 by allied commissioners War transferred to N where Taku Forts captured (20/5) and Treaty of Tientsin signed (26/6) but not ratified Public meeting (29/7) to discuss exodus of Chinese from and stoppage of supplies to H K enforced by Chinese officials led to capture of Nam Tau in San On district H K passage boat "Wing Sun" captured by pirates Much disease, Asiatic cholera and hydrophobia said to have been first introduced Violent discords in Civil Service and prosecutions of newspapers Tr. & Ind —Opium farm re-established and let for $33,000 p a Salt tax abolished P. W —Central, Western, Eastern, Tai Ping Shan, So Kun Poo (46 stalls) and Wan Chai (40 stalls) Markets constructed, all except last two abolished or superseded later Police Station No 7 erected, superseded in 1902 Leg —The Markets Ord passed this year lasted till 1887 An Ord for practitioners in law empowered barristers to act as their own solicitors Meetings of Leg Council made public (25/3)

1859.

Governor Sir Hercules Robinson, Kt, (9 9 1859 to 15 3 1865)
(Mr W T Mercer administered from 17 7 1861 to 8 9 1861 and
from 12 7 1862 to 11 2 1864)

Pr Ev —Defeat of Br fleet at the Pei Ho (25/6) and ultimatum to China (Dec) Sir J Bowring recommended annexation of Kowloon for commercial and sanitary value (29/3) and C O urged this on W O in connection with renewal of war Operation of Imp Ch Mar Customs commenced at Canton, opposed by H K merchants S S "Cumfa" plundered by pirates Agitation in England on account of disclosures with reference to Civil Service discord prejudicial to H K Ophthalmia epidemic Diocesan native training school started H K Br of R Asiatic Soc wound up and library embodied in that of Morrison Education Soc Tr & Ind —Contract Emigration confined to Br Colonies. Native boat-building greatly increased P W.—Civil hosp (9 wards with 71 beds) completed, superseded in 1874 Schools built at Shek Ho (26 scholars), Little H K (13 scholars) and Aberdeen, all subsequently given up or superseded Public station erected at Stanley. Bill to complete Praya scheme thrown out by influence of commercial houses

1860.

Pr Ev.—Renewal of war with China Chusan Is occupied (21/4), Taku Forts taken (26/8) Peking occupied (13/10) and Peking Convention (24/10) secured ratification of Treaty of Tientsin and further converted into cession a lease of the Kowloon Penin which had been obtained from Canton Viceroy on (21/3) Pawnbrokers closed their shops in ineffectual protest against new Ord P O transferred to local Govt (1/5) Great rise in value of land and consequent increase in revenue Board of Education formed for management of Govt schools (21/1) Tr & Ind —Shipping interests developed by commissariat and transport services during war P W —Tanks constructed at Bonham Road for City Waterworks Station St, Tai Ping Shan, Centre St, Second St, West St, East St, Sai Ying Pun and Peak Roads laid out Shau Ki Wan School (57 scholars) built Leg —The Pawnbrokers Ord (No. 1) regulated this business Ords constituting a marine court of enquiry and a board to grant navigation certificates were subsequently superseded

1861

Pr Ev —Emperor of China HIEN FUNG died (Jan), and Prince KUNG head of regency Occupation of Canton by allies terminated 21/10 Kowloon Peninsula formally handed over to Great Britain (19,1) and discussion with regard to military lands there at once commenced Piracy of "North Star" 4 miles out of H K Three district schools merged into new Govt Central School T, & Ind —H K Chamber of Commerce formed and establishment of Chinese Imperial Maritime Customs opposed by it P W —Accommodation for 610 Scholars provided for Central School in Gough Street Robinson Road with bridge across Glencaly laid out Police Stations built at Pok Fu Lam and Shau Ki Wan , latter superseded in 1872 Quarters for signalmen provided on Peak Lock Hosp constructed this year afterwards became part of Govt Civil Hosp

1862

P, Ft - Chinese issue of *H K Gazette* started (1,3) Registrar Gen made intermediary between Govt and Chinese Cadet system introduced by appointment of 3 student interpreters (3/4) Strike of cargo boatmen against registration under Ord of previous year Trial made of recruiting Indian police in Bombay and Madras and floating station for water police established Military opened sanitarium at Peak which proved failure Volunteer Corps consisting of battery of artillery armed with 3 prs and 4⅝" howitzers first formed (1/3) Miss P XTER started Eurasian Schools Piracies of "Henrietta Louise", "Imogen", "Eagle" and "Iron Prince" all close to H K Typhoon (27/7) resulted in considerable loss of life P W —Road from Victoria Gap to Pok Fu Lam (1½ m) laid out Timber landing piers provided at Pottinger and Ice House Streets and Observation Place Town Clock Tower (124 ft high) erected by public subscription Leg —Military Stores Ord (No 1) passed to stop supply of stores to Tai Ping rebels Volunteer, P O , and Police Ords passed this year subsequently superseded Ord empowering barristers to act as their own solicitors repealed in 1871

1863

Pr. Ev—Commission appointed to enquire into unsatisfactory working of Victoria Gaol Chair coolies struck for nearly 3 months when brought under a licensing Ord of this year Piracy of "Bertha" near Stonecutters' Island (22/7) Sailors' Home at West Point opened (31/1) Drinking fountain erected opposite City Hall site **Tr. & Ind.** —Fluctuations in value of Mexican dollar led to proposal to establish mint at H K and to make standard dollar and sub coins based on it only legal tender Messageries Maritimes mail steamers started (1/1) and regular steamer communication with Br N Borneo established (Dec) **P. W**—Reservoir (2,000,000 galls) at Pok Fu Lam, connected by aqueduct with 2 tanks above City, completed , superseded in 1871 No 4 Police Station constructed this year afterwards abolished and quarters built for Supt Bot and Afforest Dep superseded in 1892

1864

Pr Ev—Sir R Hart head of Ch Imp Maritime Customs (19/7) Tai Ping rebellion crushed by capture of Nanking (19/7) Wholesale deportation to Canton of professional beggars Many " drain-gang " and other burglaries and murderous attacks Riot of Malay seamen, police, and 99th reg (12-14/9) Piracy of " Chico " (28/1) Marine and inland lots at Kowloon sold on short leases Military contribution of £20,000 p a , estimated to be ⅕th of imp military expenditure, imposed on Colony Band (11/4), Rifle Co (24/5) and Canton Det (17/9) added to Volunteer Corps which numbered 200 active and 200 hony members at end of year Public Garden (9 acres) between Garden and Albany Roads opened (6/8) First gas lighting in Victoria (12/11) Heavy rainfall (6/6) caused collapse of houses **Tr & Ind.** —Prospectus issued in July of H K & Shanghai Banking Co , 6 banks already established at H K **P W.**—Proposal for new Praya wall and reclamation fell through owing to opposition of lot-holders Carriage road laid out to Shau Ki Wan Bowrington Canal (600′ long and 90′ wide) formed Sai Ying Pun Market (6 shops and 81 stalls) built **Leg**—Mercantile Law Amendment Ord (No 1) amended laws of trade and commerce Compilation of edition of ord in force completed (Oct)

1865.

Mr W T Mercer administered from 16 3 1865 to 10 3 1866

Pr Ev.—Project of railway to connect Calcutta with Canton and H K mooted Decided that criminals not to be extradited to China without guarantee that they will not be tortured Committee appointed to enquire into mortality of troops Board of Education abolished and Education Dep placed under Inspector who was also head of Central School St Saviour's (R C) commercial school established Piracy of " Georg Andrews " outside Lyemun Pass and of " Nuevo Lepanto " near Lan Tao **Tr. & Ind**—Union Dock Co registered (31/7) with capital of $500,000 H K , Canton & Macao Steamboat Co started (19/10) with capital of $750,000 **P** —Central Police Station (for officers and 176 constables), Victoria Gaol (120 single and 8 associated cells and accommodation for debtors), Post Office (sorting and 11 other rooms), Voluntee H Q (demolished 1905), Su Kun Pu School (for 150 scholars) and Sai Ying Pun School (for 75 scholars) completed City lighted with 400 gas lamps in March Battery Road laid out at West Point and first sections of Robinson and MacDonnell Roads in Kowloon Leg —Companies, associations and partnerships of more than 20 regulated by Companies Ord (No 1) Ords Nos 2 to 7 consolidated criminal law of H K on lines of U K Acts of 1861

1866.

Governo Sir Richard Graves MacDonnell, Kt, C.B (11 3 1866 to 11 4 1872)

(Major General H W Whitfield administered from 29 10 1868 to 12 12 1868 and from 13 4 1870 to 8 10 1871)

Pr Ev —H K Royal Mint opened (7/4), it had cost $400,000 to establish and involved annual expenditure of $70,000, commission appointed in Oct to enquire into its working System of branding and deporting criminals and flogging them if they returned to H K introduced Volunteer Corps disbanded owing to non attendance of members **Tr. & Ind** —Period of commercial depression which lasted till 1869 set in, 2 banks suspended payment H K & Shanghai Bank converted into Corporation by Ord (No 2), capital $5,000,000 H K & Whampoa Dock Co formed (11/10), capital $750,000 **P W** — Mint Buildings and Harbour Office completed, latter re-constructed in 1874 **Leg.**—The Companies Registration Ord (No 1 extended provisions of Companies Oid of previous year

1867.

Pr Ev —Commencement (15/10) of what henceforth known as Blockade of H K, Chinese cruisers patrolled neighbouring waters levying tax on junks trading with non-treaty ports, this was at first supported by British representative at Peking as means of checking smuggling from H K Commission reported in favour of closing Mint Expenditure decreased to secure balance in estimates 11 licensed gaming houses opened (15/9), afterwards increased to 16 St Paul's College (C of E) closed for lack of funds. Praya wall destroyed by typhoon (8/8) in which several large vessels and many junks lost Nearly 500 houses destroyed by fire (28/11) **Tr. & Ind** —New dock of H K & Whampoa Dock Co opened at Aberdeen (15/6) First of regular Pacific Mail S S Co's steamers from San Francisco arrived (31/1). H K Hotel Co started operations in July Two important and some smaller firms failed Exchange at 6 months' sight stood at 4/4½ on December 31st **P. W.**—Slaughter House at Belcher's Bay (superseded 1894), Governor's Peak Residence (re-constructed 1902) and Gaol on Stonecutters' Island (since abandoned) completed Land reclaimed at Kowloon Point by 500 ft of sea wall **Leg** —A Stamp Ord passed for revenue purposes, after much opposition from commercial community An Ord for the maintenance of order and cleanliness authorized licensing of gaming houses An Emigration Ord directed against abuses such as had come to light in connection with coolie emigration from Macao was subsequently strengthened.

1868.

Pr. Ev — Attempt made by Canton Viceroy to collect customs dues in H K from junks proceeding to China defeated   Agitation against licensing of gaming houses started by H K Missionaries was taken up in the U K   Mint closed after making only £20,000 in seigniorage ; buildings sold for £65,000 and plant to Japan for $60,000 (June)   Marine lot-holders successfully resisted attempt of Govt to make them re-construct sea-wall   Exchange at 6 months' sight stood at 4/4½ on December 31st   P W — Police Station No 2 built   8½ acres reclaimed by 2,700 ft of sea-wall from Wilmer St to Bonham Strand West   Leg — Amendments made to Stamp Ord   The Suppression of Piracy Ord (No 1), directed against assistance given in H K to pirates, soon had good result   Volunteer Fire Brigade established by Fire Brigade Ord (No 2)   The Treasonable Offences Ord (No 3) assimilated law on this subject with that of U K

1869

Pr Ev — The Suez Canal, destined to have great effect on H K trade a few years later, was opened on 18,3   The S of S expressed strong disapproval of raising of revenue from gaming house licences and of manner in which this revenue was used   Police Schools established   District watchmen, paid for by Chinese, first enrolled and placed under Reg Gen , immediate effect was friction between Reg Gen and Capt Supt of Police   Duke of Edinburgh visited H K (31/10 to 16/11) and opened City Hall (2/11)   Tr & Ind — Improvement in trade in spite of falling off of junk traffic due to Blockade   Messageries Maritimes and Pacific Mail doubled number of steamers and 2 new local Steamship Co s started   Exchange at 6 months' sight stood at 1 5½ on December 30th   P W — Police Station No 6 at Victoria Gap and Harbour Inspectors' Quarters built , latter afterwards given up   Leg — Proportion of unofficial to official members in Leg Council increased from 3-7 to 4·6 (25/8)   Promissory Oaths Ord (No 1) and Public Assemblages (Regulation of Traffic) Ord (No 2) passed

1870

Major General W H Whitfield administered from
13 4 1870 to 8 10 1871

P Ev — Proposal of H M Minister at Peking that Chinese consul should reside at H K opposed by Governor   Notice given by Lieut - Gov as to closing gaming houses from 1/1/71 disallowed by S of S   The Tung Wa—a Chinese free hosp to be managed by Chinese directors under Govt supervision — established by Ord (No 3)   Typhoon of 26/9 caused great loss of life and property   H K -Amoy-Shanghai (Gt Northern Co) cable opened for traffic   Tr & Ind — Commercial exploring Expedition to Kwang Tung and Kwang Si initiated by Chamber of Commerce   H K and Whampoa Dock Co absorbed Union Dock Co and increased capital to $1,000,000   Exchange at 6 months' sight stood at 4'4 on December 31st   P W — Gaol Officers' Quarters built , afterwards used mostly as gaol hosp   Leg - -Public Places Regulation Ord (No 2) passed to maintain order, etc , in public buildings, gardens and other places

1871

Pr Ev —Monopoly of gaming house licences sold (12 1) for $15,000 p m , protests from Colony and agitation in U K resulted in abandonment of licensing system (8/12) System of branding and deporting Chinese criminals and flogging them if they returned to Colony abolished (25/5) Agitation against inefficiency of police force Typhoon of 2/9 damaged houses and shipping H K -Cape St Jacques-Singapore (Eastern Extension Co) cable opened for traffic on 9 6 **Tr. & Ind** —H K Wharf and Godown Co formed Exchange at 6 months' sight stood at 4/4¾ on December 30th **P W** —Public Gardens extended by 8 2 acres between Albany Road and Glenealy Ravine Whitfield Police Station built at Causeway Bay Pok Fu Lam Reservoir (66,000,000 galls) completed for City Waterworks **Leg.**—Legal Practitioners Ord (No 1) dealt with the enrolment, etc , of barristers and attorneys

1872.

Governor Sir Arthur E Kennedy, K M C.G , C B , (16 4 1872 to 1 3 1877).
(Mr J Gardiner Austin administered from 15 10 1874 to 5 11 1875
and from 11 3.1875 to 2 12 1875)

Pr. Ev.—Board of Examiners in Chinese for Govt Officers established Gardens and Afforestation Dept placed under representative advisory committee Provision made for registering all births and deaths System of branding and deporting Chinese criminals reintroduced Coolies struck (Aug) against tax on coolie lodging-houses Bad year for malaria , dengue cases o curried for first time (Sept) St Peter's (C of E) church for seamen (14 1), Tung Wa Hosp for Chinese, and St Joseph's (R C) Church (30/11) opened Victoria Recreation Club amalgamated boat club, gymnasium and swimming bath (30 11) **Tr. & Ind** —New period of depression commenced Much discussion on Blockade of H K , and on adulteration of grey shirting in England Attempts to form brokers' association failed Commercial capabilities of West River explored 1st issue of one dollar notes by H K & Shanghai Bank (Oct) Revenue from opium farm $122,400 and Commission appointed (8/6) to enquire into working of monopoly recommended letting for 3 years instead of for 1 year as had been done since 1858 Exchange at 6 months' sight stood at 4/4 on December 31st. **P W** — Wan Chai School (for 110 Scholars), Shau Ki Wan Market (30 stalls) and Shau Ki Wan and Hung Hom Police Stations built, last superseded in **1885**

1873.

Pr Ev —Gardens and Afforestation Dept constituted sub-dept, under Surveyor Gen (15·12) Horticultural Society started for annual flower and vegetable shows (13/2) System introduced (24/4) of Govt. grants-in-aid for secular education based on result of examinations, R C schools declined to take advantage of it Victoria English School established but eventually became Portuguese (R C) First newspaper under solely Chinese management published in H K. **Tr & Ind.**—Several important commercial undertakings failed Commission appointed to consider question of Blockade of H K   Exchange stood at 4/1½ on December 31st   P W.—Yau Ma Ti Police Station built and East Praya partly constructed   Leg —Standing Rules of Leg Council revised (2/7)   Law with respect to carriage and deposit of explosives etc amended by Dangerous Goods Ord (No 1) Puisne Judge added to Supreme Court for summary jurisdiction by Supreme Court Ord (No 3) and Summary Court, established in 1871, abolished by Supreme Court (Summary Jurisdiction) Ord (No 4).

1874.

Pr. Ev —Attempts to enforce provisions for registration of servants contained in an Ord of 1866 failed   Scholarship established in connection with Govt Central School (Jan)   In typhoon of 22-23/9, 35 foreign ships, over 2,000 lives and about $5,000,000 worth of property lost in 6 hours   On other occasions 2 ships lost on rocks and 1 by collision in or near harbour   Tr & Ind —Chinese petition sent to Queen and memorial to S of S with regard to Blockade   Increased export of tea from China accompanied by complaints of adulteration   China Merchants S N Co started with design of taking coasting trade from foreign ships   H K & Shanghai Bank lent $600,000 to Chinese Government at 8% on security of maritime customs   Exchange stood at 4/1¼ on December 31st   P W.—Temporary Hosp (54 beds) provided in Holly- wood Road , it was destroyed by fire on 26/12/78   Harbour Office in Victoria re-constructed and new Harbour Office built at Aberdeen Mint Dam and Blue Pool Dam re-constructed for City Waterworks Roads and wells provided at Peak   Leg —Emigration Ord passed to supersede legislation of previous year in connection with coolie trade from Macao

1875.

Pr. Ev —Tsai Tien became, under the style of Kwong Sai, Emperor of China with the two Empresses as regents (23,2)   St Saviour's (R C) School re-organized as St Joseph's College (15/11)   Tr & Ind —De- pression in trade indicated by further failures   New proposals put forward for dealing with Blockade   Hanoi and Haiphong under French protection opened for trade (15/9)   Supply to H K of subsidiary coins from London Mint started (19/7)   Mr (afterwards Sir Thomas) Jackson Manager of H K & Shanghai Bank   Cosmopolitan Docks completed (Oct)   Exchange stood at 3/11⅞ on December 31st   P W —Light- houses at Cape D'Aguilar (1st order) and on Green Island (4th order) completed and lights exhibited on 16/4 and 1/7 respectively   30 market stalls provided at Shek Tong Tsui   Leg —Letters Patent (8/6) vested Govt in Lieut -Gov or Col Sec in event of Governor's death, incapacity or absence   Ord No 7 provided for systematic record of marriages in one general register

1876.

Pr. Ev.—Census taken. Extensive housebuilding operations on Peak. Fir trees planted on Mount Davies above Kennedy Road   Tr & Ind —Opium Farm let for 1 year from 1/3 at $110,000   Exchange stood at 4/1¼ on December 30th   P W.—Cape Collinson Lighthouse completed and 6th order light exhibited from 1/3   Kennedy Road, (1 82 m long), opened   Powder Magazine constructed at Stonecutters' Island, superseded in 1905   Leg —Chinese Passenger Ships, Public Gambling, and P O Ords , passed this year, subsequently superseded.

1877.

Governor Sir John Pope Hennessy, (22 4 1877 to 7 3 1882)
(Mr W H Marsh administered from 31 5 1877 to 6 9 1877)

Pr Ev —Public branding and flogging of criminals stopped and their deportation restricted & lenient treatment of first offenders advocated by new Governor First Chinese Civil marriage solemnized at Reg Gen 's office (7/6 First Chinese (Ng Choy) admitted to local bar (18/5) St Joseph's (R C) Cathedral re-opened for service (3/6) H K entered postal union and postage rates reduced **Tr. & Ind** —Opium Farm let for 2 years at $132,000 p a Exchange stood at 3/10⅞ on December 31st **P W** —Cattle Depôt (for 120 head) first provided at Kennedy Town Conduit, (3 38 m long), constructed to convey water from Pokfulam Reservoir to City **Leg** —Letters Patent of 9/1 revoked supplementary Charter of 8/6/75 and made minor alterations in constitution of Colony Companies Ord passed this year afterwards incorporated in No 1 of 1865

1878.

Pr. Ev.—Po Leung Kuk established by Chinese to prevent kidnapping of girls and ill treatment of domestic servant girls Many burglaries including armed attack on Chinese Bank in Wing Lok Street (25/9) Public meeting to discuss insecurity of life and property in Colony (7/10) Serious fire in Victoria 368 houses and $1,000,000 worth of property destroyed (25-26/12) Volunteer corps formed under Ord of 1862 at time of strained relations with Russia **Tr. & Ind.**—China Sugar Refinery Co , Ltd , established Exchange stood at 3/6⅜ on December 31st

1879.

Pr Ev —System of deporting criminals resumed Two thirds of police force ordered (17/3) to be always on night duty Local Committee reported on defence questions for Royal Commission at home Revision of education code confined secular system to Government schools and gave freedom to grant-in-aid schools as to religious instruction Botanical separated from Survey Department. St Patrick's Hall in Garden Road opened on 17/3 and R C Church at West Point on 22/3 Lutheran Church erected Visit of General Ulysses Grant (30/4 to 12/5) **Tr. & Ind.**—Trade depressed , much discussion on detriment to it resulting from action of Chinese revenue cruisers H K & Whampoa Dock Co. purchased ship-building slips of late Capt Sands (1/9) Opium Farm let for 3 years at $205,000 p a Exchange stood at 3/9⅞ on December 30th **Leg** —Merchant Shipping Consolidation Ord passed this year superseded in 1891

1880.

Pr Ev —Military authorities reported on insanitary condition of Colony Telegraphic communication established with Philippine Islands (1/5) Rickshaws first used in H K (22/4) Polo Club started (27/4) **Tr. & Ind.**—Cosmopolitan Dock Co established at Sham Shui Po (3/2) but their dock subsequently (31/12) purchased by H K & Whampoa Dock Co H K. Ice Co registered (31/2) Exchange stood 3/9¾ on December 30th. **P W** —Additional block erected at Govt Civil Hosp.

originally used for Lock Hosp **Leg**—Naturalisation Ord giving European resident (E J EITEL) privileges of British Subject within Colony but not elsewhere, passed this year, formed precedent frequently followed afterwards

1881

Mr M S Tonnochy administered from 11 9 81 to 24 10 81

Pr Ev.—Census taken Speculation in land and house property resulted in considerable increase in Colonial revenue Severe gale (14/10) damaged small craft in harbour 36 houses destroyed by fire in Tai Ping Shan (19/1) Telephones taken into use in Colony First issue of "Hongkong Telegraph" newspaper (15/6) Visit of Prince ALBERT VICTOR and Prince GEORGE of Wales (20/12 to 31/12) Exchange stood at 3/8¼ on December 31st **P W**—A smaller proportion of the public revenue devoted to Public Works than in any year since 1851 and no works of importance in hand Leg—Macao Extradition Ord (No 1) provided for apprehension of fugitives from justice from Macao

1882

Mr William Marsh, C M G, administered from 8 3 1882 to 29 3 1883

Pr Ev—Previous year's speculation in land and house property followed by numerous bankruptcies Mr O CHADWICK, C M G, reported as Sanitary Commissioner on sanitary condition of Colony Enrolment of Volunteers in new Artillery Corps commenced (20/12) **Tr & Ind.**—Luzon Sugar Refinery Co established (25 3) Opium Farm let for 1 year at $210,000 p a Exchange stood at 3/7⅜ on December 30th **Leg**—Banishment and Conditional Pardons Ord (No 1) enabled Gov-in-Council to banish aliens for 5 years New Volunteer Ord superseded Ord of 1862

1883

Governor Sir George Ferguson Bowen, G C M G,
(30 3.1883 to 19 12 1885)

Pr. Ev—Sanitary Board first established Disturbance among hawkers owing to enforcement of new regulations (22/5) Belilios Scholarships instituted (29/11) New St Joseph's (R C) College for boys inaugurated (6/1) The Peak Church (C of E) opened (17 6) H K connected by cable with Shanghai (29/5) and Foochow (18/6) Canton-Kowloon Telegraph Line opened for traffic (9/7) **Tr. & Ind.**—Opium boiled at Govt Factory and Dross Farm let Exchange stood at 3/8¾ on December 31st **P W**—Breakwater, 1,400 ft long, constructed at Causeway Bay to provide safe anchorage of 100 acres for small craft Observatory at Kowloon completed **Leg**—Distress of Rents Ord (No 1)

1884.

Pr. Ev.—War broke out between France and China (5 8) and gave rise to some unrest in Colony. Piratical attack on S S "Greyhound" a few hours out of H K Strikes of butchers (10 6) and of cargo-boat people and coolies (3/10) Serious fires at Hung Hom in Br Kowloon (11 and 16/12) Jockey Club formed (4/10) Hongkong-Macao cable opened for traffic (4 7) Tr & Ind —Opium boiled at Govt Factory and Dross Farm let Exchange stood at 3/6½ on December 31st P. W —European Lunatic Asylum (8 cells, etc) constructed near Govt Civil Hosp 23 acres reclaimed at Causeway Bay Water Police Station and Time-ball Tower erected at Tsim Sha Tsui Yau Ma Ti Market extended (30 stalls) Leg —Medical Registration Ord

1885.

Sir William Marsh, K C M G, administered from 20 12 1885 to 25 4 1887

P Pv —Peace declared between France and China (6,4) allayed unrest Agitation with regard to overcrowding of City of Victoria led to appointment of Land Commission Tr & Ind —Ropeworks established at Kennedy Town Opium Farm let for 1 year at $159,000 Exchange stood at 3/4½ on December 31st P W.—Police Boat Basin (0 43 acre) with launch slip and boat shed constructed at Tsim Sha Tsui and Police Station at Hung Hom Leg —Weights and Measures Ord (No 2), Bills of Exchange Ord, modelled on English Act, (No 3), and Married Women (Disposition of Property) Ord (No 5) passed Municipal Rates Ord, subsequently modified, fixed rates at 13% for Victoria (police 8¾, lighting 1½, fire-brigade ¾ and water 2), at 8¾ % for the Peak, at 6 % for Kowloon, etc

1886

Pr Iv —Land Commission recommended reclamation by Govt Agreement (11/9) with China by which movement of opium to and from H K was to be registered and arrangements made for settling disputes between H K junks and Chinese Customs put a stop to so called H K Blockade which had been detrimental to trade Tr & Ind —Opium Farm let for 3 years at $182,400 p a Exchange stood at 3,5¼ on December 31st P W —22 acres reclaimed at Kennedy Town by sea-wall 3,690 ft long Lazaretto for 4 Europeans and 16 Chinese) constructed on Stonecutters' Island Loan of £200,000 at 4½ % for carrying out public works raised by issue of debentures Leg —Royal Instructions of 11/10 revoked previous and enacted new instructions official members of Leg Council fixed at 7, unofficial at 5 Printers and Publishers Ord (No 4) regulated printing of newspapers and books Usury Ord (No 5) made 8 % legal rate of interest Bills of Sale Ord (No 7) passed to prevent fraud on creditors and Peace Preservation Ord (No 10) for prevention and suppression of riots

1887

*Major General W Gordon Cameron, C B, administered
from 26 4 1887 to 5 10 1887*

Pr Iv —Chinese School of Medicine founded Alice Memorial Hosp (London Missionary Society) for Chinese opened (17/2) Exchange stood at 3/1¼ on December 31st P W —Police Stations erected at Kennedy Town (subsequently used as Infectious Diseases Hospital and Mount Gough Leg —Defamation and Libels Ord (No 1) passed Triad and other Unlawful Societies suppressed No 2) Jury Ord (No 5) amended and consolidated law relating to Jurors and Raw Opium Ord (No 9) better regulated trade in opium

1888.

Governor Sir William Des Vœux (6 10 1887 to 7 5 1891)
(Mr Frederick Stewart administered from 7 3 1888 to 20 3 1888, from
24 11 1888 to 18 12 1888 and from 30 8 1889 to 23 9 1889)

Pr Ev —Sanitary Board reconstituted under a Public Health Ord of previous year and Colonial Surgeon made president Bad year for small-pox, 99 cases being admitted into hospital Wire-rope tramway, commenced 20 9 85, from St John's Cathedral (100 ft) to Victoria Gap (1,300 ft) opened for traffic (30 5) Exchange stood at 3 0½ on December 31st P W —Cattle Depôt at Kennedy Town extended for 240 additional head Leg —Letters Patent of 19/1 revoked Charter of 5/4/43 and Letters Patent of 9/4 77 and re-enacted provisions for govt of Colony Royal Instructions of 19 1 revoked those of 11 1 86 and re-enacted them with slight modifications Regulation of Chinese Ord (No 3) provided for registration of householders and tenants, for appointment of District Watchmen, for regulation of ceremonies, etc , and for issue of night passes Coroner's duties transferred to Magistrates by Coroners Abolition Ord (No 5)

1889.

Pr Ev —33 11 inches of rain fell in great storm of 29/5 and 30/5 (16 16 in 7 hours) and did considerable damage Tr & Ind —Opium Farm let for 3 years at $447,600 p a Exchange stood at 3/1¼ on December 31st P W —Queen's College, commenced in 1884, completed and provided accommodation for 924 scholars, subsequently increased Original Tytam Scheme for City Waterworks completed and provided impounding reservoir (312,330,000 galls), tunnel (1 38 m long), conduit (3 m long), 6 filter beds (3,245 sq yds agg area), and service reservoir (5,700,000 galls), total capacity of storage reservoir now 378 330,000 galls Leg —Chinese Emigration regulated by Ord No 1 and law of evidence consolidated by Evidence Ord (No 2) Praya Reclamation Ord (No 6) provided for extensive reclamation in front of West Praya at cost of Marine lot-holders Chinese Extradition Oid (No 7) gave effect to Art XXI of Treaty of Pekin

1890.

Mr Francis Fleming, C M G , administered from
19 2 1890 to 22 12 1890

Pr Fv.—Visit of Duke and Duchess of Connaught (April), Duke laid memorial stone of Praya Reclamation The Scheme initiated by Mr (afterward Sir) PAUL CHATER was to reclaim 65 acres extending 2 miles from Naval Yard to beyond Gasworks at West Point , new road along front to be called Connaught Road Lighting of low levels in Victoria by 50 arc lamps begun 1/12 Piracy of Passenger S S "Namoa" 50 m from Hongkong (Dec) Exchange averaged 3/2 for the year and stood at 3 5 on December 31st P W.—Pokfulam filter beds (4), with area of 1,360 sq yds , constructed for City Waterworks Leg —Law relating to infant vaccination amended by Vaccination Ord (No 2) and those relating to jurisdiction, etc , of Magistrates by Magistrates Ord (No. 3) Merchandise Marks Ord. (No. 4) framed on lines of English Act.

1891.

Major-General Digby Barker administered from 7 5.1891 to 9 12 1891

Pr. Ev —Census taken **Tr & Ind** —Fluctuation in exchange and speculation mostly in trading and mining ventures outside Colony resulted in financial depression Exchange averaged 3/4¼ for the year and stood at 3/1 on December 31st **P W** —Foreshore at Kennedy Town (8 55 acres) reclaimed Lunatic Asylum for Chinese (16 cells, etc) near Civil Hosp , District School at Sai Ying Pun (for 186 scholars), and new Police Station at Aberdeen erected The Peak, previously dependent on well water, now supplied from City Waterworks by pumping **Leg** —Gambling Ord (No 2) passed to stop gambling among Chinese, and Companies (Sale of Shares) Ord (No 5) to stop gambling in shares Bankruptcy Ord (No 7) brought law of Colony into line with that of U K Opium Farm regulated by Prepared Opium Ord (No. 8)

1892.

Governor Sir William Robinson, K C M G , (10 12 1891 to 1 ? 1898)
(Mr G. T. M O'Brien administered during absence
of Governor in 1893)

Pr. Ev —State aid withdrawn from Church of England in Colony, and Cathedral handed over to trustees Gas lighting introduced at Kowloon **Tr. & Ind.**—Opium Farm let for 3 years at $340,800 p a Exchange averaged 3/1¼ for the year and stood at 2/8¼ on December 31st **P. W** —Gap Rock Lightho completed and connected with H K by cable , 1st order light exhibited 1 4 City Waterworks distribution scheme completed 10 Public Laundries opened at Wan Chai Cattle depôt at Kennedy Town extended for 120 additional head Albany Nullah trained. Govt. ho. ball-room, new quarters, etc , for Supt B & A Dept & staff quarters (for 11) at Govt Civil Hosp completed Hosp Ship "Hygeia" (since abolished) opened (Aug) **Leg** —The Patents Ord (No 2)

1893.

Pr. Ev.—Heavy fall in silver seriously affected public expenditure and new 3½% loan of £200,000 raised for carrying out certain public works School for girls on site of former Central School, with accommodation for 608, presented by Mr E R BELILIOS, taken over by Govt The Po Leung Kuk, a Chinese institution for the protection of women and children, formed in 1878, incorporated Volunteers organized as a field battery and machine gun company Waglan Lightho completed by Chinese Govt ; light exhibited 9/5 Exchange averaged 2/8¼ for the year and stood at 2/3 on December 30th **Leg.**—Volunteer Ord (No 4) superseded Ord of 1882 Nethersole Hosp (London Missionary Society) for Chinese women opened (5/9)

1894.

Pr. Ev —Some trouble caused by clan fight in March First outbreak of bubonic plague, at its height between May and July, produced temporary exodus, estimated at 100,000, and great interference to trade

War between China and Japan, declared 1/8, for a time partially paraly-
zed Chinese markets   Caterpillar plague injured pine tree plantations
Typhoon of 5/10 did some damage in harbour   £140,000 of the 1836
$4\frac{1}{2}\%$ loan of £200,000 converted to $3\frac{1}{2}\%$ at cost of £1,800 and balance of
£60,000 redeemed from sinking fund , total loan now £341,800 of
$3\frac{1}{2}\%$ stock   Hong Kong-Labuan (Borneo)-Singapore cable opened for
traffic 4/5   Exchange averaged 2 2 for the year and stood at 2 - on
December 31st   P W.—New Slaughter Houses provided at Kennedy
Town. Roads laid out in E of Kowloon.

1895.

Pr Ev.—Strike as protest against new lodging house regulations
lasted from 23/3 to 4/4 , on 27/3 over 20,000 coolies out   **Tr & Ind**
—New British dollar introduced   General improvement in local stocks
and undertakings   Opium Farm let for 3 years at $296,000 p a   Ex-
change averaged $2/0\frac{3}{4}$ for the year and stood at $2 1\frac{5}{8}$ on December 31st
P W —Resumption of insanitary properties at Tai Ping Shan com-
pleted   Central Market (138 shops and 150 stalls), commenced 1890, and
Gaol extension (155 cells, etc), commenced 1893, completed   Additional
4,400,000 gallons impounded at Pokfulam for City Waterworks , total
capacity of storage reservoirs now 382,730,000 gallons   At Kowloon
original waterworks to supply 250,000 gallons a day from 3 wells N of
Yau Ma Ti opened, Macdonnell Road extended to N , Cattle Depôt (112
head) built at Hung Hom, and Signalling Station established at Black-
head's Hill   Leg —The Private Vehicles Licensing Ord (No 5)

1896.

Pr Ev.—In second plague epidemic 8 Europeans died but dis-
location of business much less than in 1894   Commission appointed
to report on insanitary dwellings   Military contribution of Colony fixed
at $17\frac{1}{2}\%$ of gross revenue exclusive of capital expenditure on works and
buildings   Typhoon of 29/7 caused considerable damage to property
Tr. & Ind —Unprofitable year for trade, importations except of flour and
kerosine oil being on limited scale and sales generally unsatisfactory
Exchange averaged $2/2\frac{1}{4}$ for the year and stood at $2/1\frac{7}{8}$ on December
30th   **P. W.**—Streets laid out at Tai Kok Tsui. **Leg** —Additional
Royal Instructions of 7/7 substituted O C Troops for Ch Justice on Leg
Council and increased number of Unofficial Members from 5 to 6   British
North Borneo Extradition Ord (No 1) passed   Factors Ord (No 3)
and Sale of Goods Ord (No 4) introduced *mutatis mutandis* provisions
of English Acts

1897.

Pr. Ev —Area at Causeway Bay set apart as Queen's Recreation
Ground   **Tr & Ind.**—Trade on the whole unsatisfactory and adversely
affected by fluctuations in exchange and scarcity of money   Exchange
averaged $2/0\frac{3}{4}$ for the year and stood at $1/11\frac{11}{16}$ on December 31st   **P W** —
For City Waterworks Tytam dam raised to impound additional 94,670,000
galls , total capacity of storage reservoirs now 477,400,000 galls
Maternity Hosp. provided at Govt Civil Hosp. **Leg.**—Partnership Ord
(No 1) on lines of U K Act, Probate Ord (No 2), Protection of
Women and Girls Ord (No 4) and Vagrancy Ord. (No 9)

1898.

Major-General Wilsone Black, C B , administered from 2 2 1898 to 24 11 1898

Pr Ev —Penny post established By convention between U K and China, signed at Peking on 9/6, area on the mainland S of line joining Deep Bay with Mirs Bay (270 sq m) together with Lantao and other islands (90 sq m) leased to Great Britain for 99 years , this area designated The New Territories **Tr & Ind** —West River opened for trade on 3 6 and regular communication established but interfered with by piracy Import trade of Colony improved particularly in rice and coal Opium Farm let for 3 years at $372,000 p a. Exchange averaged 1 10½ for the year and stood at 1/11 2/5 on December 31st **P. W.**—1893 loan fully expended Tai Ping Shan improvement scheme completed. Barker Road (5,660 ft long) and Chamberlain Road (2,340 ft long) opened on Peak Tai Kok Tsui Market (32 stalls) erected **Leg.**—Registration of Trade Marks Ord. (No 6) and Liquor Licences Ord (No 8)

1899.

Governor Sir Henry Arthur Blake, K C M G , (25 11 1898 to 21.11 1903)

Pr Ev —New Territories taken over by hoisting British flag at Tai Po on 16·4 , on account of opposition including attack on Br Troops by some 2,600 Chinese on 19·4, in which Chinese authorities were believed to have connived, Sham Chun City beyond new boundary occupied from 16/5 to 13/11. 2 machine gun, 1 infantry and 1 engineer companies added to Volunteers **Tr. & Ind** —Hongkong Cotton Spinning, Weaving & Dyeing Co started operations (1 6) Green Island Cement Co previously at Macao commenced manufacture at Hok Un near Kowloon for local use and export Sugar refineries did well. Exchange averaged 1/11½ for the year and stood at 1/11 7/8, on December 27th **P W** --Laying out of streets at Mong Kok Tsui, N of Yau Ma Ti, begun Wong Nei Cheong Reservoir (33,994,000 galls) completed for City Waterworks , total capacity of storage reservoirs now 511,394,000 galls **Leg** --N T Exemption of Laws and Regulation Ords (Nos 6 and 8) for administering N T , Prisons Ord (No 1), Criminal Procedure Ord (No 9), Merchant Shipping Ord (No 10) supplementary to English Acts, and an Ord , afterwards superseded, for sanitary regulation of buildings

1900.

Pr. Ev —H K served as Br. base during Boxer troubles in the North In typhoon of 9/11 H M S "Sandpiper", 10 launches and over 110 junks sunk and over 200 lives lost in 3 hours Soldiers' Club opened (14/4). **Tr. & Ind.**—Chinese Customs placed difficulties in way of river steamers trading with West River Ports Output of granite from Shau Ki Wan and Kowloon quarries estimated at $45,000 and $80,000 respectively Cotton Spinning Co experienced difficulties on account of labour supply Exchange averaged 2 4·099 for the year and stood at 2/1 1/8 on December 31st **P W.**—Blake Pier (200' × 40') built. City Disinfecting Stn completed Signalling Station established on Green Island, and Waglan connected by cable with H K Wong Nei

Cheong Recreation Ground extended   Police Stations erected at Tai Po,
Sha Tau Tok, Au Tau and Ping Shan in N. T and connected by
telephone   **Leg.**—N T Extension of Laws and Land Court Ords
(Nos 4 and 8) for administering N T, P O Ord (No 6), and
and Police Force Ord (No 11)   New Edition of the Statute Laws
of the Colony put in hand by Sir J CARRINGTON

1901.

Pr. Ev.—Census taken   Plague mortality higher than in any year
since 1894 and S of S petitioned to send out Sanitary experts to
investigate   **Tr & Ind.**—Import trade depressed   Cotton Spinning
Co wrote down shares and brought in fresh capital   Opium Farm let
for 3 years at $750,000 p a   Exchange averaged 1/11 4005 for the year
and stood at 1/10⅝ on December 31st   **P W**—Associated converted
into single cells and new block (78 cells) constructed at Gaol   Police
Station erected at Sai Kung in N T   **Leg.**—Defence Contribution Ord
(No 1) raised annual military contribution of Colony from 17½% to 20%
of gross revenue   Code of Civil Procedure (No 3) regulated procedure
in Supreme Court   Another Ord , afterwards superseded, was passed for
sanitary regulation of buildings   Trustees Ord (No 5) and Fine Arts
Copyright Ord (No 18) were on lines of U K Acts   Rating Ord (No 6)
left rates at Victoria at 13% and raised them to 10¾% at the Peak, 12¼%
at Kowloon and 7 to 10½% at other places

1902.

*Major General Sir W J Gascoigne, K C M G , administered
from 4 1 1902 to 8 9 1902*

Pr. Ev— Mr O CHADWICK & Prof SIMPSON reported on Sanitation
of Colony   Committee on Education made various recommendations
including more instruction in Chinese   Penny letter postage extended
to Br Agencies in China   Volunteer Corps re-organized into 2 Artillery
and 1 Engineer Co   **Tr. & Ind**—Manufacture of rattan furniture for
export started on large scale by American firm   Cotton spinning did
better than in previous years, sugar refining worse   Exchange averaged
1 8 6724 for the year and stood at 1 7₁¼ on December 31st   **P W.**—
Governor's new Peak Residence completed   New quarters provided
for gaol staff (6 married and 40 single Europeans and 56 Indians)
Police Stations erected in Victoria (No. 7), at Sheung Shui in N T , and
at Tai O in Lantao.   New Kowloon Water Works commenced (Apl)
Leg.—Four Ords dealt with land in N T   Water-works Consolidation
Ord had for its object economizing of water

1903.

Pr. Ev.—New Education Code made grants dependent on results
of inspection and not of annual examinations.   New wing of Tung Wa
Hospital opened   Letters to Europe first sent by Siberian Railway
(13/10).   **Tr. & Ind.**—Brussels Sugar Convention coming into effect

1/9 improved condition of sugar refining industry High price of raw
cotton prejudicially affected cotton spinning Exchange averaged
1/8 5243 for the year and stood at 1 8½⅞ on December 31st P W —
Victoria Hosp for women and children (44 beds) on Peak and 16 ft
road from Kennedy Town to Aberdeen (5 m) handed over by Jubilee
Committee Ladder Street Resumption Scheme completed 1st public
bath-house (40 baths) opened at Wanchai Conduit Road (2,900 ft
long) opened N T Survey completed New Government Offices commenced (June) Foundation Stone of the New Law Courts laid (12/11)
Leg.—The Public Health and Buildings Ord (No 1) superseded all
former Ord s dealing with this matter and made extensive and minute
provision for improving health of Colony Waterworks Ord (No 16)
repealed Ord of previous year and made other provisions for economizing water supply Four Ord s dealt with land in N. T

1904.

Mr F H May, C M.G., administered from 22 11 1903 to 28 7 1904

Pr. Ev.—Outbreak of war between Russia and Japan (8 2) brought
influx of colliers, etc and decrease of foreign ships Speculation resulted
in heavy losses among Chinese Attempt to start emigration of indentured
labourers to S Africa failed owing to local opposing interests and was
abandoned after shipment of 1,746 Land Court determined 354,277
claims to land in N T, where there was evidence of increasing
prosperity Mounted troop added to Volunteers and Vol Reserve
Association established. **Tr. & Ind** —Cotton spinning did badly at
commencement but better at end of year Sugar industry brought large
profits to refineries Opium Farm let for 3 years at $2,200,000 p a
reduced to $2,040,000 p a from 1/11 3′ 6″ El Tramway from Kennedy
Town to Shau Ki Wan (9½ m) opened for traffic Exchange averaged
1/10 07176 for the year and stood at 1/11⅝ on December 31st
P. W —Praya Reclamation completed Tytam Byewash Reservoir added
26,301,000 galls to storage for City Waterworks , total capacity of storage
reservoirs now 537,695,000 galls Kennedy Town Cattle Depôt extended
to hold 1,241 head 2nd public bath-house (38 baths) opened at Tai
Ping Shan Gascoigne Road at Kowloon and 14 ft road to Tai Po
(16 m) in N T. completed New Rifle Ranges provided behind Kowloon
City **Leg** —Sugar Convention Ord (No 14) forbad importation of
bounty fed sugar Pilots Ord (No. 3) provided for exam and licensing
of Pilots. Hill Dist. Reservation Ord. (No. 4) reserved residential area
at the **Peak**

1905.

Governor Sir Matthew Nathan, K C M C., 29 7 1904 to 20 4 1907.

Pr. Ev.—Russo-Japanese war and especially proximity of Russian
fleet (April–May) and subsequent sinking of Br S S. "Oldhamia" (18/5)
and "St Kilda" (4 6) gave rise at H K to various questions as to duties
and rights of neutrals Before signature of armistice on 1/9 shipping
tended to return to normal conditions Govt of H K on 2/10 lent the
Hu Kwang Viceroy £1,100,000 repayable in 10 annual instalments for
redemption of Canton-Hankow Railw concession. Unsuccessful negotia-
tions carried on through year in connection with Ch. section of Canton-

Kowloon Railway   Parcel post arrangement with Germany came into force (1/6) and postage to Australia reduced (15/7)   Revised rent roll introduced in N T   Anglo-Chinese Govt School opened at Aberdeen   **Tr. & Ind.**—Trade adversely affected by over-speculation in 1904, by fluctuations in exchange, by boycott of American goods as protest against U S A exclusion law and by reduction of Br fleet in China   Imports to and exports from China fell off   Sugar refineries, Cotton Spinning Co and cement and rope factories did good business   There was falling off in repairing and docking ships   Exchange averaged 1/11 2335 for the year and stood at 2 0⅝ on December 30th   **P. W**—Preliminary Survey of Br section of Canton-Kowloon Railway carried out, route selected and land partly resumed   Construction was commenced under P W D at the latter end of the year   1st order light from Cape D'Aguilar transferred to new tower at Green Is   Disinfecting Stn at Kowloon, Mong Kok Tsui Market (40 stalls) and Yau Ma Ti District School (for 200 scholars) completed   Resumption scheme finished at Kau U Fong (27,156 sq. ft) and commenced at Mee Lun Lane   900 ft Robinson and Gascoigne South roads extended   **Leg**—12 (including 4 financial and 6 amending) Ords passed of which most important were N T Land Ords (Nos 3 & 9) for facilitating land transfers and settling land disputes

1906.

Mr F H May, C.M.G, administered from 15 12 1906 to 23 1 1907

Pr. Ev.—Commission appointed to enquire into administration of Sanitary Laws (28/4)   The construction of the Kowloon-Canton Railway (British Section) was taken over by the Construction Staff appointed by Consulting Engineers in May   The Beacon Hill tunnel was commenced, South face (15/9) North face (1.12)   Piracy of British Steamer "Sainam" on West River, British Missionary killed (13/8)   Severe typhoon (18/9), 15 European including Protestant Bishop and some 10,000 Chinese drowned, 2,413 Chinese craft reported lost, 141 European vessels and launches foundered or badly damaged   British Steamer "Hankow" burnt at wharf, 111 lives lost (14/10)   Census taken (6/11)   Kowloon-Canton Railway Final Loan Agreement signed (10/11)   **Tr. & Ind**—General depression in trade , heavy losses through fall in price of Indian yarn , shares in local undertakings much depreciated in value.   Increased importation of Australian flour   Iron mining started and a large Flour Mill opened in the New Territories   Exchange averaged 2/1 7064 for the year and stood at 2/3 1/8 on December 29th   **P. W.**—Harbour Office, Western Market, Bacteriological Institute, Volunteers' Headquarters, Taipo Quarters, and Gunpowder Depôt completed   Considerable progress made with Kowloon roads and extension of Conduit Road in Victoria , Mee Lun Lane resumption scheme well advanced , new Kowloon Reservoir brought into use and rider main system completed   **Leg**—17 Ords passed including Married Women's Property and Criminal Evidence Ords (Nos. 5 & 14) designed to bring local law into line with English statutes

1907.

*Governor Sir Frederick John Dealtry Lugard, K.C.M.G., C.B.,
D S O, 29 7 1907.*

(*Mr F H. May, C M G administered from 21.4.1907 to 28.7.1907*)

Pr Ev.—Commission appointed to enquire into administration of Sanitary Laws reported (19/3) Claim for compensation, on account of lives lost in "Sainam" piracy, settled. Survey of Chinese Section of the Kowloon-Canton Railway commenced H.R.H the Duke of Connaught accompanied by H.R H the Duchess of Connaught and Princess Patricia of Connaught visited the Colony (6/2). Sir M. Nathan appointed Governor of Natal ; succeeded by Sir F. J. D. Lugard, who was appointed 1 5 and arrived in Colony 29/7 **Tr. & Ind.**—Continued depression of trade accentuated towards the end of the year by world-wide restriction of commerce following upon financial crisis in America. Shipping in particular suffered The local sugar industry held its own but shares in the majority of local undertakings further depreciated in value A project to start a Brewery made headway Development of iron mining in N T arrested. Tin smelting increased Assessment made in July for year 1907-8 showed that rateable value for whole Colony had decreased by 2·52% Opium Farm let for 3 years at $1,452 000 p.a. Loss and inconvenience caused by depreciation of subsidiary currency and over-issue of sub coin by the Canton Mint Exchange averaged 2 1·8499 for the year and stood at 1/9¼ on December 31st **P. W.**—The Tytam Tuk Waterworks (1st Section) were practically completed affording a further permanent storage of 195,914,000 gallons and of 210,370,000 with movable weir added A Mortuary at Kowloon and a Market of 68 stalls at Quarry Bay were completed also the extensions to Conduit Road East and West, the first extension of the Kowloon City Road towards Customs House Pass and a further extension of Robinson Road Northwards. The Mee Lun Lane resumption scheme was also finished **Leg.**—16 Ords. (5 amendment) passed ; Hongkong College of Medicine incorporated , H.K. & S. Bank authorized to increase its capital from ten to twenty million dollars and to continue incorporated for a further term of 21 years ; Life Insurance Companies Ord passed

1908

Pr. Ev.—Mr H. N Mody offered to present Colony with buildings necessary for a University : Committee formed to promote the undertaking and collect endowment fund Instructions received from H.M. Government that all opium divans in Colony must be closed. Disastrous Typhoon on the night of 27th to 28th July. Riot in town of Victoria on 1st and 2nd November in connection with boycott of Japanese goods by the Cantonese **Tr. & Ind** —Money plentiful owing to lack of remunerative employment No sign of revival in the real estate market. Import business on the whole showed some improvement on the preceding years in spite of the downward tendency of exchange and the growing tendency of trade to go direct to Canton. The sugar refining industry showed better results The Cotton Mill had a poor year. The shipping industry shared in a world wide depression in the carrying trade, and this was reflected locally in a marked falling off in the business of the Dock Company All export business and especially silk suffered as a result of the great financial crisis in America Loss by depreciation of subsidiary currency continued, the Government withdrew from circulation and demonetized $780,000 of subsidiary silver coin and $30,000 of bronze coin Exchange averaged 1 9 6727 for the year and stood at 1,8⅜ on December 31st P W —The new Time Ball Tower was completed and brought into use. A section of the new Land Office at Tai Po was completed for the use of the Assistant Land Officer. The new Slaughter Houses and Animal Depôt at Ma Tau Kok, Kowloon were completed and brought into use. The extension of P.W D Offices was carried out Wanchai School was extended and its accommodation practically doubled Sarjmgpun School was also enlarged by the erection of an additional storey. The Quarters at the Victoria School had another storey added The European Quarters in Mount Gough Police Station were considerably enlarged. The Transvaal Coolie Emigration Depot was purchased for a Quarantine Station and buildings etc put in order Staff Quarters in Government Civil Hospital were extended. Obelisk at Kowloon in memory of the French sailors drowned in Typhoon 1906 was unveiled. 12 New Fire Alarms were installed in City Nathan Road was extended from Market Street to Kowloon Farm Lot No 2 In New Territories the Kowloon City Road was extended from its point of intersection with the Military Roads to its point of bifurcation to Customs Pass and Chin Lan Chun Village. Blake Pier Permanent Shelter was completed New Service Reservoir at West Point was completed capacity 418,000 gallons ; also a new 8″ rising main to Peak Leg —22 Ordinances (9 amendment) passed the principal matters dealt with were—public health and buildings, fire insurance companies, foreign corporations, breweries, chemists and druggists and theatres. Public Health and Buildings bill passed after much debate and permanent Head of Sanitary Dept created (result of Commission) Chinese Emigration Ordinance 1889 amended and "assisted emigrants" recognised, affording additional protection and safeguards Small Debts Court instituted in N.T , and Widows' and Orphans' Pension Fund transferred to Hongkong Government.

1909.

Pr. Ev.—International Opium Conference at Shanghai (Feb). 26 opium divans in H.K. closed (1,3). The headings from each end of Beacon Hill tunnel met (17/5). Opium Ordinances amended and consolidated in accordance with the resolutions of the Shanghai Conference, additional restrictions and safeguards being imposed in respect of morphine, compounds of opiums and cocaine (1/9). Duties imposed on intoxicating liquors (17 9) Very severe typhoon (19-20/10). Conference held in H.K between Portuguese and Chinese Commissioners for delimitation of boundaries of Macao (June-Nov.). Total endowment fund of proposed H.K. University amounted at close of year to $533,496 exclusive of $718,614 promised. **Tr. & Ind.**—The local money market was easy throughout the year Real estate showed faint signs of revival In imports a large business was done. Exports were active, silk in good demand. The sugar refining industry prospered.

Shipping showed a slight improvement on the previous year, but this was not reflected in the local docking industries which suffered from insufficient work. Loss by depreciation of subsidiary currency continued the Govt withdrew from circulation and demonetized $779,712 of subsidiary silver coin and $40,646 of bronze coin. Exchange averaged 1 9 0601 for the year and stood at 1 9‚% on Dec 31st. **P. W.**—The old stables adjoining the Government Offices were extended and raised to render the upper storey available and so provide additional accommodation for the staff of the Public Works Department A bungalow on the mainland at Tai Po for the Assistant District Officer was completed. A staircase from the ball-room to the grounds of Government House was constructed A road from Ma Tau Kok to Tai Shek Kn was completed; the level of Des Vœux Road, Kowloon, (re-named Chatham Road), was raised , and arrangements were made for the construction of a new road traversing Marine Lot 29 from Queen's Road East to Praya East. The old fish pond at Tai Wo Shi (N.T) was filled in The Albany Filter Beds were reconstructed and extended and the filtering area increased from 3,246 to 4.945 square yards Extensive resumptions of land at Kowloon Point were effected with a view to providing a site for the terminal station of the Kowloon-Canton Railway Public latrines were constructed at Tai Kok Tsui, in Chuk Hing Lane, at Wongneichong Village and adjoining Kennedy Road to the westward of the Peak Tramway Ping Shan—Shataukok Road surveyed and part constructed. **Leg** — 46 Ordinances (32 amendment) passed · the principal matters dealt with were—opium, liquor, trade marks, railways. and the construction of a harbour of refuge at Mongkoktsui.

1910.

(Sir F H May, K C M G , administered from 30 4 10 to 31 10 10)

Pr Ev.—All opium divans in H.K. and the N T. closed (1 3) Opium Farm let for 3 years at $1,183,200 p.a (1 3) H B.M.'s Government make the Colony a grant of £9,000 for the year 1910 on account of loss of opium revenue. Foundation stone of H.K. University laid by Sir F. D Lugard (16 3) Endowment fund of University stood at $1,239,828 (exclusive of $96,460 promised) on 31st Dec. Considerable scarcity of water owing to dryness of the season, but heavy rains in June removed anxiety. Plague cases decreased to 25, the lowest since 1897. Trouble at Macao with pirates on Colowan Island: Portuguese troops and gunboats engaged many pirates escaped, some afterwards arrested at Chenng Chau Island in the N.T. (July). British Section, Kowloon-Canton Railway, opened by Sir Henry May (1/10). Portuguese Republic proclaimed in Macao (10.10) **Tr. & Ind.**—The local money market was easy during the first 6 months of the year, but afterwards inclined to be tight, owing probably to the fall in rubber stocks. Financial crisis in Shanghai caused by rubber boom , many banks failed (Aug./Sept.) In imports of raw sugar there was a heavy falling off due mainly to producers in Java sending direct to Northern markets without trans-shipment in H.K. There was also a falling off in import and export of raw opium due partly to an additional tax on opium imposed, contrary to treaty, by the Canton Government Compounds of opium including morphine also declined due to restrictive legislation by Government The year was fair generally for merchants and manufacturers; yarn, piece-goods, and tin did well The number and tonnage of ships entering and clearing in the Colony was the largest yet recorded, being 545,177 vessels of 36,141,496 tons, an increase as compared with 1909 of 17,897 vessels and 1,610,651 tons. There was a considerable improvement in the industry of docking steamers in H.K during the latter part of the year the industry gained a considerable impetus, which has since been maintained Subsidiary currency remained at a discount: the Government withdrew from circulation and demonetized $5,272,012 25 (face value) of silver sub-coin and $255,446.79 (face value) of copper coin Exchange averaged 1/9 60216 for the year and stood at 1/10 on 31st Dec. **P. W.**—A new block containing 78 cells was constructed in Victoria Goal An extension of the Land Office at Tai Po for the accommodation of the District Officer was completed. A small slaughter house for Shaukiwan District was built at Sai Wan Ho Argyle Street, Kowloon, was extended eastwards as far as the Railway to afford access to Yaumati Station and the diversion and alteration of Chatham and Gascoigne Roads on account of the construction of the Railway were completed In the N T. the road from Castle Peak Bay was completed as far as Un Long and the extension from San Tin Village to Au Ha Gap was well advanced The large nullah west of the University site was trained. Ferro-concrete piers at Kowloon City and at the Gunpowder Depôt, Green Island, were completed Causeway Bay was deepened to 1 foot below low water. The Kowloon Water Works Gravitation Scheme, begun in 1902, was completed. A 12″ main for conveying Tytam Water to the Western district of the City was laid in Caine Road The sites of several houses which had collapsed in Morrison Street were acquired in connection with the re-construction of the Old Western Market and further extensive areas were resumed at Kowloon Point to provide a site for the terminus of the Railway **Leg.**—34 Ordinances (21 amendment) passed · Ordinances relating to the N T. consolidated the principal other matters dealt with were—copyright, crown suits lepers, midwives, oaths, and volunteer reserve.

	TRADE		FINANCE										POPULATION		
			REVENUE		EXPENDITURE	MILITARY EXPENDITURE	PERCENTAGE OF EXPENDITURE DEVOTED TO						EXPENDITURE PER HEAD			
	IMPORT	TONNAGE	Local	Imperial			Non clero Charges	General Administration	Public Health	Public Instruction	Public Order	Public Works		Non Chinese	Chinese	TOTAL
			£		£	£							£			
1841															5,600	
1842															12,361	
1843																
1844	538	189,257	9,035	54,234	58,108	152,343		24 38	1 64	2 40	21 11	50 17		454	19,009	19,463
			63,769													
1845	672	226,998	22,212	52,545	72,841	148,100		26 22	1 23	1 18	26 10	45 32	529	1,043	23,114	24,157
			74,757													
1846	675	229,200	27,047	29,223	60,851	141,781		29 81	1 16	1 26	32 44	35 80	1,075	1,386	20,449	21,835
			54,270													
1847	641	229,465	31,079	18,394	60,969	117,119		29 88	1 51	1 82	33 27	34 52	2,240	1,406	22,466	23,873
			49,473													
1848	701	258,818	25,072	40,302	62,309	80,778		27 55	1 46	1 82	29 83	40 34	2,076	1,502	22,496	23,998
			65,374													
1849	802	293,165	28,617	11,910	38,986	75,943	57	40 97	3 11	2 04	47 25	1576	3,116	1,210	28,397	29,507
			39,527													
1850	883	299,009	28,527	11,150	34,314	64,628	38	44 74	3 16	1 97	41 64	8 11	2,812	1,305	31,987	33,292
			37,677													

TRADE				FINANCE											CLI
SHIPS ENTERED			EMI GRANTS LEFT	REVENUE		EXPENDITURE	MILITARY EXPENDITURE	PERCENTAGE OF EXPENDITURE DEVOTED TO						REVENUE DERIVED FROM RATES	TEMPER.
Number	Tonnage	Percentage of British Tonnage		Local	Imperial			Non religious Charges	General Administration	Public Health	Public Instruction	Public Order	Public Works		Maximum
				£	£	£	£							£	o
1,052	377,084			23,721 / 20,154 — 43,875		34,115	51,896	06	43 72	2 67	2 66	42 52	8 85	2,959	
1 097	433,383			21,381 / 22,000 — 43,381		34,766	50,395	05	36 84	2 09	2 70	39 58	17 74	2,326	
1,103	477,063			21,700 / 9,500 — 31,200		36 413	50,346	14	36 49	2 78	1 83	49 60	19 16	2,705	93
1,100	413,354			27 045 / 5,966 — 33,011		34,635	41,541	03	33 89	2 05	3 17	41 90	18 93	3,327	
1,736	604,580		14,683	47 974		40,314	34,830	1 21	28 40	1 50	2 15	39.02	27 72	3,917	89
2,091	811,307		14,130	35 500		42,426	99,823	15	27 12	1 43	2 36	43 90	24 99	5,868	91
1 070	541,063			58,842		65 498		33	26 03	1 23	1 93	38 10	32 38	7 377	
Entered & Cleared															
1,975	1,354,173	54	15,810	62,476		52,979	234,814		24 71	1 87	2.60	37 82	32 91	13,281	91
2,179	1,164,640	42	10,217	65,225		66,109	267,468	54	23 02	4.03	3 07	39 76	29 55	14,047	90.50
2,838*	1,565,645	46	15,183	94,183		72,391		79	25 69	4 79	2 53	36 09	31 12	16,573	

* Exclusive of Canton & Macao River Steamers

		FINANCE										CLIMATE			POPULATION			PUBL
EMI RANTS LEFT	REVENUE	EXPENDI TURE	MILITA Y EXPEN DITURE	PERCENTAGE F EXPENDITURE DEVOTED TO						REVENUE DERIVED FROM TAXES	TEMPERATURE		RAINFALL	NON CHINESE	CHINESE	TOTAL	DEATHI FOR ANNUM
	Local | Imports			Net Cost (Largest)	General Admini ration	Public Health	Public Instruc tion	Police Action	Public Works		Maxi mum	Mini mum					
	£	£	£							£	o	r	Ins				
	23,721 20,154	34 115	51,866	06	19 72	2 67	2 68	42 52	8 35	2 969				1 620	31 463	32,983	
	43,875																
	21,831 22 000	34 766	50 398	05	36.84	3 09	2 70	37.58	17 74	2 326				1 041	35,517	37,058	
	43,831																
	24,700 9,500	50,419	50,346	14	36 49	2 78	1 83	39 50	19 16	2,705	93	43	78.95	2,481	37,536	39,017	
	34,200																
	27,046 5,965	34,685	41,541	03	33 49	2 06	3 17	41 00	18 96	3,327			96 59	1,643	54 072	55 715	
	33,011																
14,683	17 974	40 814	38,830	1 21	28 40	1 50	2 16	8 02	27 72	3,917	89	49	100 55	1,956	70,651	72 607	
14,180	35,500	42 426	39,823	15	27 11	1 48	2 86	43.90	2' 99	3,868	91	42	119 42	2,479	69,231	71 730	
	58,842	65 498		33	26 04	1 23	1 97	38 10	32 38	7 377			81 68	1 411 Whites	75,683 Coloured	77,094	
15,810	62,476	52,979	237,814		24 71	1 97	2 69	67 82	32 91	18,251	91	50	76 58	1,462 Non Chinese	74,041 Chinese	75,503	
10,217	63,225	68 109	267,463	04	24.02	4 03	3.07	39 76	29 58	14,047	90 50	47	83 59	1,661	85,280	86,941	
16,183	91,183	72,391		1 79	25 69	4 79	2 53	35 09	31 12	16,573			99 72	2,476	92,441	94,917	

TRADE					FINANCE											
SHIPS CLEARED AND ENTERED			EMIGRATION				PERCENTAGE OF EXPENDITURE DEVOTED TO							EXCESS OF ASSETS OVER	REVENUE DERIVED FROM
Number	Total Tonnage	Percentage (British) Tonnage	Left	Remained	REVENUE	EXPENDITURE	Non-effective charges	General Administration	Public Health	Public Instruction	Public Order	Public Works	Miscellaneous	LIABILITIES (+) OR OWED LIABILITIES OVER ASSETS (−)	RATES
														$	£
2 545	1 310 383	41	12 810	16	£127 241 £107 692 or 610 759 52 274	} 39	30 67	2 91	1 56	27 76	4 66		+ 394 600	1 756
2 720	1,344,710	46	10 421	7 188	611,260 587,519	1 36	20 23	2 94	1 76	33 65	40 0		+ 475 439	19,096 (880,097)
3,657	1,806,881	52	7,400	7,19	576,379 596 569	1 70	22 52	2 60	1 84	42 42	4 92		+ 140,000	27,331
4,558	2,046,372	55	6,607	6,778	637,846 763 308	1 11	16 66	2 20	1 63	30 12	48 05		+ 298,190	25,519
4,445	2,134,164	60	6,849	6,626	844 444 937,805	1 01	22 54	1 86	1 37	25 13	40 01	7 68	+ 184 107	17,024
3,783	1,891 281	55	5,116	9,263	769,077 996,953	1 47	32 72	1 99	1 28	26 82	40 51	10 21	+ 24,606	12,464
4 879	2 376,320	63	4,283	9 886	839,404 780,917	2 16	36 71	2 68	1 68	38 80	18 88		+ 25,851	16,440
														RATEABLE VALUE OF COLONY $	
4,093	1,974 299	62	9,701	10,752	1,134 106 991,311	1 69	26 19	2 35	1 43	27 18	19 16 21 62		+ 137,365	1,512 265
4,426	2,206,049	58	18,285	10,207	923,653 912,853	1 82	29 72	2 71	1 83	31 60	24 17	9 95	+ 123,031	1,756,077
4,791	2,640,347	62	12,992	16,618	914,976 877,224	2 09	25 65	3 34	2 16	29 77	26 31	10 69	+ 64 117	1,676,319

FINANCE									CLIMATE			POPULATION			PUBLIC HEALTH
	PERCENTAGE OF EXPENDITURE DEVOTED TO						EXCESS OF ASSETS OVER LIABILITIES (+) OR OF LIABILITIES OVER ASSETS (−)	REVENUE DERIVED FROM RATES	TEMPERATURE						DEATH RATE PER 1,000
M	Total effective Charges	General administration	Public Health	Public Instruction	Public Order	Public Works	Defence			Maxi-mum	Mini-mum	AVERAGE	NON-Chinese	Chinese	TOTAL	European & American Residents
								$	£	°	°	Ins				
332 / 334 }	2 39	20.07	2 94	1 96	27 78	44 66		+ 393 600	15 756	90	46	78 56	2,986	116,635	119 321	64 3
534	1 36	20.23	2 94	1 76	35 64	40 06		+ 475 439	19 096 ($95,007)	92	42	91 01	3,034	120,477	123,511	22 4
565	1 70	22 52	2.60	1 84	42 42	28 92		+ 143,000	27,331	91	50	81 61	3,149	120 701	124,350	63.2
308	1 14	16 66	2 20	1 53	30 42	48.05		+ 298,190	25,519	90	41	94 09	3,630	117,868	121 498	55 5
305	1 01	22.84	1 86	1 37	25 23	40.01	7 66	+ 184,107	37,024	90	49	56 36	4,007	121,497	125,504	49 1
355	1 47	32 72	1 99	1 28	25.82	26 51	10 21	+ 24,606	42,564	93	45	77 49	3,616	111,482	115,098	35 0
317	2 16	30 71	2 68	1 68	38 89	18 88		+ 25,851	46,140	92	41	80 80	3,636	113,835	117,471	26.0
311	1 69	26 19	2 25	1 46	27 43	19 46	21 52	+ 137,365	RATEABLE VALUE OF COLONY $ 1,642,265	88	42	83 04	No Estimate made of population			19.0
553	1 82	29 72	2 71	1 83	31 60	24 17	9 95	+ 128,031	1,755,077	89	45	6,371	7,099	114,280	121,979	29 2
524	2 03	25.65	3 34	2 16	29 77	26.31	10 69	+ 154,117	1,676,349	90 5	46	5,607	8,754	115,444	124,198	31 0

TRADE					FINANCE											
SHIPS CLEARED AND ENTERED			EMIGRATION		REVENUE	EXPENDITURE	PERCENTAGE OF EXPENDITURE DEVOTED TO								EXCESS OF EXPENDITURE (+) OR REVENUE OVER EXPENDITURE (—)	RATEABLE VALUE OF COLONY
Number	Total Tonnage	Percentage of Entries Tonnage	No. of	Estimated			Non effective Charges	General Administration	Public Health	Public Instruction	Public Order	Public Works	Defence		
	$				$	$									$	$
?	3,289,701	?	9,501	19 754	844,178	894,209	2 07	24 80	4 04	2 15	30 97	26.07	10 40	+ 120,099	1,662,647
6 099	3,795,066	63	27 721	23 73	921 807	835,696	2 35	25 ...	3 25	2 4	30 54	19 94	10 87	+ 16 ,942	1,620,979
4,670	3,973,119	67	28 765	25,300	847,834	789 874	1 96	26 73	4 06	2 78	36 19	16.43	11 68	+ 235,335	1 676,032
5,356	3,034,016	68	31,866	32,319	864,800	921,480	2 00	26 60	3 59	2 86	29 66	25 02	10 40	+ 156 177	1,682,057
5,201	3,893,687	72	48,152	38,602	896,684	869 825	1 72	25 70	4 13	3 04	32 81	21 3	11 25	+ 192,498	1,668,410
5,751	4,359,516	72	46,850	42,390	885,309	902,500	1 54	25 49	4 85	2 85	31 50	24.62	11 76	+ 134 237	1,607,871
5,701	4,850 896	76	39,741	46,746	1,005,312	873,208	1 57	25 20	4 18	2 84	32 57	23 66	11 5	+ 310,103	1,732,186
6,131	5,909,437	74	38,653	47,882	947,838	910,523	2 82	27 29	14 72	3 41	30 71	19 53	11 50	+ 300,034	1,754,662
5,503	4,964,859	76	33,529	50,542	964,095	926,668	2 78	27 99	4 59	3 72	32 06	17 02	11 84	— 190,204	1,900,870
6,775	5,078,868	74	50 324	51,011	1,069,948	945,014	2 69	31 04	5 41	3 84	31 79	14 04	11 11	+ 275 652	2 093,460

		FINANCE								CLIMATE			POPULATION			PUBLIC H	
		PERCENTAGE OF EXPENDITURE DEVOTED TO						EXCESS OF ASSETS OVER LIABILITIES (+) OR LIABILITY OVER ASSETS (−)	RATEABLE VALUE OF COLONY	TEMPERATURE			INCREASE			DEATH RATE PER	
ENUE	EXPENDITURE	Non-effective A.Land Changes p stion	General Health	Public Instruction	Public Order	Public Works	Defence			Maximum	Minimum	RAINFALL	BIRTHS		TOTAL	Europeans and American Residents	Chinese
$	$							$	$	°	°	Ins					
1,118	394,309	2 07	24 30	4 04	2 15	30 97	26 07	10 40	+ 120,099	1,662,547	80	16	99 24	No Estimate made of population			30 8	N rec ava
1,807	885,698	2 30	23.0	3 20	2 41	30 51	19.01	10.0	+ 18,942	1,620,979	99 8	43 5	62 92	6 421	115,564	121,985	2o 0	
7,324	799,804	1 96	26 73	4 03	2 78	30 19	16.03	11 68	+ 235,385	1,676,052	91	49	75 47				19 4 Non Chinese	
8,800	921 480	2 09	26 69	3 58	2 56	29 66	25.02	10 40	+ 150,177	1,682,057	90	47	84,98	No Estimate made of population			22 2	31 9
8,624	869 823	1 82	25 70	4 13	3 04	32 81	21 09	11 25	+ 199 199	1 668 410	91	41	83 43				28 18	25 7
8,309	902,000	1 51	23 39	3 35	2 80	31 50	24 62	11 76	+ 184,237	1,657,871	90	37	108 55	8,976	130,168	139 144	24 45	28 39
5,312	873,208	1 07	26 20	4 18	2 84	32 97	22 05	11 59	+ 310,108	1,734,196	95	41	76 72				18 0	27 41
,638	910,523	2 82	27 29	1 72	3 41	30 71	19.55	11 50	+ 300,034	1,764,662	95	38	84 40	No Estimate made of population			18 7	30 35
,096	926,868	2 78	27 99	4 09	3 72	32 06	17 02	11 64	+ 190,254	1,900,870	94	45	94 70				18 1	33 11
,948	948,014	2 69	31 09	2 41	3 84	31 79	14.08	11 11	+ 275,652	2,095,460	95	39	111 57				16 71	29 51

TRADE						FINANCE										
SHIPS CLEARED AND ENTERED			EMIGRATION					PERCENTAGE OF EXPENDITURE ON DUTIES							EXCESS OF ASSETS OR LIABILITIES (+) OR (−) OR OF LIABILITIES OVER ASSETS (−)	PUBLIC LIABILITIES NOT INCLUDING REVENUE FUND	AMOUNT PAID OF TOTAL
Number	Total Tonnage	Per cent British Tonnage	Left	Returned	REVENUE	EXPENDITURE	Non effective Charges	General Administration	Public Health	Public Instruction	Public Order	Public Works	Defence			
					$	$									$	£	$
6,412	5,696,438	74	70,625	52,983	1,324,456	981,582	2 98	30 73	5.65	3 95	31 7	14 05	11 67	+ 663 710			2,005,1
6,880	6,637,024	76	78,864	61,905	1,209,017	1,094,905	3 54	27 96	5 38	4 67	29 71	19 45	9 99	+ 1,148,064			2,304,8
6,785	6,842,381	71	57,485	74,722	1,289 442	1 342,299	2 16	24 17	4.62	3 93	24.60	32 29	8 34	+ 1,067,201		No Public Debt	2,380,0
6,601	6,951,758	77	51,247	73 767	1,173,071	1,595,398	1 93	24 75	4 43	3.09	22 73	36 63	7 40	+ 729,962			2,404 3
6,827	7 699,099	78	57,517	80,773	1,251 890	1,621,250	2 24	23 40	3 44	3.67	20 76	39 85	7 24	+ 427,692			
8,448	9,080,390	74	64,522	88,704	1,367,978	2,020,862	2 09	20 93	3.04	2 47	17 08	48 94	6 16	− 191,62 2	200,000		2,900,9
8,162	9 169,534	74	52,897	92,375	1,427,456	2,023,902	4.37	19 19	3 10	2 46	18 13	46 23	6 32	+ 631 734	176 464		2,900,6
7,581	9,005,677	72	56,195	98 196	1,507,800	1,992,380	7 93	24.96	3 56	2 77	18 26	37 17	6 76	+ 360 690	189,302		3,042,2
7,688	8,971,990	74	17,649	99,816	1,928,749	1 833,719	8 23	23 32	7 32	3 28	20 24	30.30	7 32	+ 506,110	182,420		3,283,2
9 219	9,771,743	72	42,066	101,147	1,995,220	915,3 0	7 38	24 82	7 72	3.91	19 17	40 19	6 21	+ 309,732	175,248		3,768,0
8,707	10,273,043	70	45,162	105,199	2 025,303	2,449,088	6.03	20 06	6 15	3 23	15.99	31 55	17 19	+ 231 178	165,947		3,749 1
8,974	10,294,152	74	52,144	97,971	2,236,983	2,342,887	7 98	23 03	7 65	3 85	18.40	28 34	11 48	+ 93,106	157,242		3,630,9
8,758	10,537,859	74	42,366	106,644	2,078,185	1,920,524	13 20	24 96	8.46	4 17	20 21	13 01	15 97*	+ 1,469,023	118,282		3,637 6

* Expenditure on loan for Public Work

		FINANCE												CLIMATE			POPULATION			PUBLIC
		PERCENTAGE OF EXPENDITURE DEVOTED TO							EXCESS OF ASSETS OVER LIABILITIES (+) OR OF LIABILITIES OVER ASSETS (−).	PUBLIC DEBT LESS ACCUMULATED SINKING FUND.	RATEABLE VALUE OF COLONY.	TEMPERATURE.							DEATH-RATE
REVENUE.	EXPENDITURE.	Non-effective Charges.	General Administration.	Public Health.	Public Instruction.	Public Order.	Public Works.	Deferred				Maximum.	Minimum.	RAINFALL	Non-Chinese	Chinese	TOTAL.	Non-Chinese	Chinese
$	$								$	£	$	°	°	Ins.					
,324,456	981,582	2.93	30.73	5.45	3.95	31.77	14.05	11.07	+ 663,710		2,095,139	96.0	40.0	98.21	9.712	150,690	160,402	18.22	24.4
,209,517	1,094,805	3.54	27.96	5.24	4.07	29.71	19.45	9.99	+1,148,664		2,308,882	95.0	38.0	73.13				15.75	26.7
,289,448	1,342,299	2.16	24.17	4.62	3.93	24.50	32.28	8.51	+1,067,201		2,330,010	98.0	40.0	117.20		No Estimate made of population.		17.60	30.8
,175,071	1,555,398	1.93	24.75	3.43	3.09	22.75	36.65	7.40	+ 729,562		2,404,802	91.8	43.0	76.42				16.57	27.5
,251,890	1,521,250	2.24	23.40	3.44	3.07	20.76	39.85	7.24	+ 427,692		3,451,717 (to 35.8.85) 2,319,944 (to 30.8.86)	89.3	45.0	108.92				20.90	38.11
367,978	2,020,862	2.09	20.23	3.03	2.47	17.08	48.94	6.16	− 191,512	200,000	2,590,942	89.7	41.8	69.17	10,412	171,290	181,720	18.54	26.6
427,486	2,023,002	4.57	19.19	3.10	2.46	18.13	46.23	6 32	+ 631,734	196,464	2,900,698	90.7	42.8	66.20	10,522	175,410	185,962	23.51	28.90
557,800	1,962,336	7.22	24.26	3.56	2.77	18.26	37.17	6.76	+ 360,650	189,382	3,042,201	92.9	40.6	101.58	10,682	179,580	190,222	25.28	32.25
823,349	1,833,719	8.23	23.32	7.32	3.28	20.23	30.30	7.32	+ 505,110	182,320	3,283,279	92.5	40.3	119.72	10,832	183,650	194,482	17.54	31.00
995,220	1,915,350	7.38	24.82	7.72	3.91	19.47	20.19	6.51	+ 309,732	175,248	3,768,027	93.8	44.0	70.93	10,972	187,770	198,742	17.13	23.21
923,305	2,449,086	6.03	23.06	6.15	3.23	15.99	31.83	17.19	+ 231,178	165,947	3,749,121	92.9	41.8	117.12	10,494	214,320	224,814	18.20	24.18
236,933	2,343,837	7.36	23.03	7.56	3.85	18.40	28.32	11.48	+ 85,106	157,242	3,530,946	93.9	41.2	90.97	10,590	221,072	231,662	17.37	31.30
778,135	1,920,524	13.20	24.96	8.48	4.17	20.21	13.01	15.97*	+1,489,023	148,232	3,637,648	92.5	32.0	99.96	10,686	228,038	238,734	17.97	23.93

* Expenditure on loan for Public Works in this year not included in calculation of percentage.

TRADE					FINANCE												
Ships engaged in Foreign Trade (Cleared and Entered)			POPULATION		REVENUE	EXPENDITURE	PERCENTAGE OF EXPENDITURE DEVOTED TO									EXCESS OF ASSETS OVER LIABILITIES (+) OR OF LIABILITIES OVER ASSETS (−)	PUB DEBT PER HEAD OF POP.
Number	Total Tonnage	Percentage of British Tonnage	Left	Returned			Net effective Charges	General Administration. Do	Sittings of Govern't	Public Health	Education	Public Works	Public Works	Defence				
					$	$											$	£
8,452	10,469,232	75	149,023	90,095	2,278,528	2,299,096	14.00	30.39		7.41	3.5	17.06	11.01	16.57			+1,498,513	341
9,089	11,625,528	71	73,139	112,680	2,186,229	2,572,373	7.51	22.40		5.92	2.08	12.98	16.79	12.77			+55,374	341
9,352	12,593,370	71	66,829	119,468	2,609,879	2,474,910	9.91	26.24		9.06	4.16	16.72	13.77	21.14			548,964	340
9,944	12,124,590	67	62,641	115,207	2,685,915	2,641,410	11.29	27.97		8.78	2.81	15.09	16.01	18.05			2,57,	336
11,058	13,292,733	66	60,432	105,441	2,918,159	2,841,805	11.54	27.25		8.27	2.61	18.82	18.24	18.27			+313,338	332
10,905	13,483,147	65	61,075	110,448	3,510,148	3,162,792	10.43	31.10		8.04	2.43	11.06	13.41	20.54			−311,773	329
10,940	14,022,167	65	63,643	121,322	4,202,587	3,628,447	8.42	25.75		7.65	2.25	15.92	21.54	18.07			+1,100,786	325
10,967	14,599,141	58	65,774	129,030	4,213,894	4,111,722	8.28	26.35		7.55	2.16	15.00	19.96	1.569			+1,030,125	321
12,461	16,275,998	59	71,711	128,812	4,901,073	5,909,549	6.47	27.64		8.66	1.59	11.21	30.22	16.16			+65,270	316
14,982	17,018,411	59	83,384	140,451	5,238,858	5,396,669	7.26	17.64		12.70	2.46	16.00	25.38	18.51			−62,711	312
16,976	19,381,096	70	73,304	149,190	6,848,045	6,570,235	5.84	14.13		10.16	2.43	13.42	33.40	20.62			+297,783	307
18,101	19,775,176	67	64,341	140,483	6,915,434	6,951,275	5.25	17.66		9.40	2.33	12.17	32.75	20.44			+441,496	305
16,317	19,833,666	61	70,725	134,912	7,035,012	6,832,611	4.87	20.55		9.65	2.89	12.19	34.54	19.86			+652,230	1,443
18,096	20,781,421	51.5	100,96	140,822	6,602,286	5,757,203	5.46	17.97		11.27	3.20	14.72	25.50	21.88			+1,411,749	1,485
19,504	20,104,795	58.6	71,081	137,809	6,104,207	5,929,478	6.73	15.89		8.82	2.59	11.20	39.38	16.41			+1,073,01,	1,42.
18,714	20,171,755	56.7	77,430	144,851	6,822,960	6,543,830	4.96	19.09		9.89	3.35	14.45	29.52	19.32			+1,358,1600	1.39
17,557	20,965,504	57.5	111,004	149,564	6,960,869	6,907,113	6.32	11.53	7.88	8.56	3.37	13.83	28.15	20.36			+1,401,924,06	1,38.

p to 1909, Post Office was included in General Administration

	FINANCE										CLIMATE			POPULATION			PUBLIC H
	PERCENTAGE OF EXPENDITURE DEVOTED TO							EXCESS OF ASSETS OVER LIABILITIES (+) OR OF LIABILITIES OVER ASSETS (—)	PUBLIC DEBT LESS ACCUM. FUNDED SINKING FUND	CAPITAL VALUE OF RLY	TEMPERATURE						DEATH RATE PER
	Non Li Charges	General Administ t'n tot	Under taking bel or ment	Public Health	Public Instr tn	Pub Works	Defence				Max idue	Min mum	RAINFALL	NON CHINESE	CHINESE	TOTAL	Non Chinese	Chi nese
								$	£	$	°	°	In*					
6	11 00	30,39		7 41	3 o1	17 86	1 0i	1o 87	+1 142,o,1o	941 90	3 398 25 8	92 0	41 4	104 2o	10 7 2	23,224	246,006	23 28	30 42
3	7 51	22 40		7 92	2 08	12 96	35 79	12 2	+ 587 17	641,800	3 991 912	91 0	43 5	45 43	10,8 9	23 ,670	248,498	17 64	21 92
0	9 91	26.91		9 66	3 16	16 72	15 7	2 11	51 904	340,205	3 82,749	94 0	47 7	79 78	12,100	226,710	239 419	19 9	24 70
0	11 29	27 97		8 73	2 83	15 09	15.0	15 05	2,5.1	336 625	4,1 ,50	91 8	41 0	100.09	13,700	236,010	248,710	14 89	9 08
15	11 51	27 21		8 27	2 61	13.82	18 24	18 47	+213,3 1	332,945	4 521 917	91 5	46 1	57 02	15 190	239,210	254,400	19 15	22 0
12	10 42	31 10		8 04	2 43	14 00	13 41	20 14	311,7 1	32 117	4,986,831	92 9	43 o	72 70	15,832	243,490	259,312	15 23	24 40
17	8 82	26 75		7 65	2 25	15 92	21 o4	18 07	+1,100,786	520 311	5 896 391	97 3	31 6	78 73	14 77	247,900	262,678	20 14	25 10
22	8 28	26.85		7 56	2 16	15.00	19 96	23 69	+1,036 25	214 30	6,884 7 4	92 7	34 4	55 79	20,096	280,544	300,660	20.50	23.77
19	6 47	27 64		6.66	1 59	11 95	30.22	16 16	+ 66,970	315 709	8 156,615	92 2	45 5	97 50	18,524	293,300	311,824	19 00	21 95
19	7 26	17 61		12 70	2 46	16.05	25.38	18 51	62 711	412 147	8 749,843	92 4	41 9	93 66	18,591	307,0 1	325,631	16 16	9 19
10	5 84	14 19		10 16	2.43	13 42	33 40	20 62	+ 297,723	307,424	9 950 021	91 1	41 8	80 41	18 900	342,306	361,206	12 49	17 18
5	5 25	17 06		9 40	2 53	12 17	32 75	20 14	+ 441,196	30 ,270	10,472 278	91 3	42 8	70 95	17 977	359,87	377,850	11 06	17 46
1	4.89	20 53		9,55	2 89	12 19	30 54	19 50	+ 652 146	413 149	10,06 9 18	93 7	46 8	7 80	21,550	307,388	329,038	14 02	26 41
13	5 45	17 97		11 27	2 20	14 72	25 40	2. 88	+1 444 719	1,485,733	10,716 17	9 1	45	93.52	18 570	395 818	414,368	15 46	22 52
8	6 73	15.39		8.12	2 99	11 23	39 58	6 31	+1,073 041	1,42 5029	10 750 909	92 6	14 7	91 88	13,786	401 713	421 499	14 78	23 95
9	4.86	19.09		9.39	3 35	14 45	29 51	19 32	+1 113 169	5 889 159	10,7 60,902	93 8	49 7	7o 72	20,479	408,409	428,888	12 45	21 68
8	6 42	11 53	7 88	8 66	5 27	13.83	28 15	20 49	—1 490 424 9	1 787,971	11 09. 17 9	91 3	14 2	70 2	20 90	415 180	435,86	10 0	22 60